CHRISTIANS

AND

NIGERIAN POLITICS

BY

REVD. EFFIONG A. ESEDEKE

Wipf & Stock
PUBLISHERS
Eugene, Oregon

Wipf and Stock Publishers
199 W 8th Ave, Suite 3
Eugene, OR 97401

Christians and Nigerian Politics
By Esedeke, Effiong A.

ISBN: 1-57910-826-1
Publication date 1/23/2002
Previously published by Effort Printers Nigeria, 2000

DEDICATION

This book is dedicated to all the Nationalists who staked their lives for the independence of Nigeria.

To visionary leaders and pragmatic Christians who are interested in the development of Nigeria.

And

To my miracle son – Master Onwiabasi Effiong Esedeke.

ACKNOWLEDGEMENTS

My special thanks and appreciation to God Almighty and Jesus Christ my saviour who had given me abundant grace to be what I am today.

A very special thanks to my elder Sister Arit Asuquo Esedeke for her numerous support in all aspect of my life and our family.

Thanks to Chief Dr. Edet J. Amana who sponsored my university education as a father and mentor.

To Chief Okon Abia Bassey who took great pain to go through the manuscript and editing the write-up. I also say thanks to Mr. Okpoyo Etifit, a co-editor.

I will like to thank my very special friend, Rev. Uche Kalu Ibe, for his encouragements and Rev. Ini Ukpuho for his advice on how I should best handle the work. Thanks to all my colleagues in Trinity Union Theological College for their great encouragement. To the students of T.U.T.C., Umuahia.

My special regard also to my beloved wife, Mrs. Comfort Effiong Esedeke, the "best woman" I know in my life.

I also want to thank Mr. Daniel O. Dike Mr. Kalu Ire and James Fred for typing the manuscript and typesetting the work.

To the Ven. Owen Azubuike through whom this work is published.

Finally, I am sincerely very grateful to all of you. God bless you all.

FOREWORD

The author of the book, "Christians And Nigerian Politics,"is a clergyman, a lecturer in Trinity Union Theological College, Umuahia and more than any other thing, a Christian.

Like the prophets of old, he has a burden in his heart. His worry is not the multi-ethnicity and religious pluralism of Nigeria of which he is aware but the inability of Christian Politicians to play their role as "light of the World and salt of the earth (Matt.5,13-14). It is not only that many have failed to influence society but worse still, they are in the band wagon of corrupt practices – one of the factors of under-development of the nation.

He asks questions and offers answers by way of suggestion after sighing over the appalling state of the society. In the Old Testament the prophets had a hard time showing old Israel that they had failed their God-given responsibility of being witnesses in the social life of the people. So the Holy Spirit is telling Christians, the New Israel to live up to Divine expectation. Socio-political injustice whether done by Israel, the Bible says in 1 John 4:17 "...as He (Jesus Christ) is, so are we in this world." This has socio-political implications, like the statement of "light" and "Salt" already quoted. Christians are like Jesus in love and God who is Love lives in us by the power of the Holy Spirit. Before His execution, Jesus boldly denounced wrong religious teachings and practices. He was challenged by the Herodians about the payment of tax to Rome. His positive reply is in Mark 12:17. Therefore Christianity should uphold government while condemning the sinfulness of men which corrupts the system. The author re-awakens his fellow Christians to their responsibilities because Christians exist to exercise beneficial influence on society as a whole. This is because the place for the salt is not in the salt-cellar, any more than the place for the lamp is under a bucket. Christians, like their Master, are in Nigeria as those that save. I recommend the book to all Colleges of Theology and to all practicing Christians.

Rev. Canon Prof. V. N. Uzoho

Rector of Trinity Union Theological College,

Umuahia.

WORD OF WISDOM

DO NOT IMAGINE THAT YOU IN THE KING'S PALACE, ASO ROCK VILLA, GOVERNMENT HOUSE, NATIONAL ASSEMBLY, HOUSE OF ASSEMBLY, LOCAL GOVERNMENT CHAIRMEN AND COUNCILORS, HIGH GOVERNMENTAL AND POLITICAL OFFICE CAN ESCAPE ANY MORE THAN ALL THE NIGERIANS.

FOR IF YOU REMAIN SILENT WITHOUT PRAGMATIC ACTION AT THIS TIME, RELIEF, AND DELIVERANCE WILL ARISE FOR THE NIGERIANS FROM ANOTHER PLACE AND YOU AND YOUR FATHER'S HOUSE WILL PERISH (REMEMBER ABACHA). AND WHO KNOWS WHETHER YOU HAVE NOT ATTAINED ROYALTY, ADDRESSED AS HIS EXCELLENCY, HONOURABLE, GIVEN AUTHORITY AND POWER FOR SUCH A TIME AS THIS?

(ESTHER 4:13-14 NASB)
AMPLIFIED BY THE AUTHOR
FOR NIGERIANS.

Table of Contents

CHAPTER ONE

"Happy is the nation whose God is the Lord, the people whom He has chosen as His heritage" (Psalm 33:12)

INTRODUCTION

This book is a treatise that deals mainly with the 'Christian' in relationship with the political problems of our country, Nigeria. It is an attempt to find the Christians highest order with regards to attitude, manner or conduct and most general reason which justifies their action or what their position should be in the area of Nigerian politics.

I know that there are Christian books or literatures that may have treated Christian and politics but the arguments in this book are those, which no Christian must miss to read carefully. I am not saying the above out of my rhetorical power.

> ***. The scriptures have over the years been misquoted, church divided and fellowship broken because of a mere mention of the word 'POLITICS'***

It is my delight that Christian(s) should

not continue as complainants in the Nigerian society. There are quite a lot of factors that seem to be dragging Nigeria backward in politics and through these factors, politics in the Nigerian context is basically considered to be dirty, if not a very dirty game. Some nomenclatures to which Christians have developed phobias on the mention of such word would be considered.

Christians both in quote or underline are followers of Christ their master and they believe that the world belongs to God Almighty whom through Christ is their father. Therefore they have specific roles to play in earthly things in order to take the world through their direction. For over ten years I have been inclined so much into knowing what is happening in the world as a global village, the role of some Christians, so-called or real, in the political affairs of their country. The scriptures have over the years been misquoted, church divided and fellowship broken because of a mere mention of the word 'POLITICS.' The scripture is going to be our yardstick as we go through this book.

> *All scriptures is inspired by God and*
> *is useful for teaching, for reproof, for*
> *correction, and for training in righteous*

ness, so that everyone who belongs to God may be proficient, equipped for every good work (2 Tim.3:16, 17 NRSV)

Within the Christian fold are to be found about four groups of people with four different views or standpoint about 'Christian' and politics. The first set are the hardcore fundamentalists or extremists whose opinion about politics is that Christians should have nothing to do with elected public offices or positions. To this group it is nonsensical for any Christian to think about anything that has to do with politics. It is a sin to talk about politics in their mist and to be a partisan politician.

The second group is the one, which is made up of 'I don't care people.' This is 'I don't care group, 'with their 'I don't care attitude' towards anything political. So long as the word 'politics' is mentioned, their position is that of being neutral. Neutral in the sense of not knowing what their role should be, as Christians. Like people in the first group, they do not fail to complain about some bad government, politics and governance but then, theirs is that they do not know whether they should turn to the right or left. They do not know their privileges and fundamental Human Rights. My final designation for them is "anything goes.

Thirdly, we have a group that is a little bit midway They stand both for and against politics political affairs or politics. On one hand, people in this group appreciate the lower cadre of Christians to be involved in politics while the higher cadre – the elders, leaders and Pastors of the churches should not have a say in anything political. Some of the questions raised by this group are: can any serious Christian be a politician? Politics is too dirty for any church leader or pastor. How can a church leader or a pastor be involved in such a dirty game? Can a Christian be a politician and still be a Christian? In other words, politics is only for the so-called Christians and not for the real Christians.

> ***"can any serious Christian be a politician? Politics is too dirty for any church leader or pastor"***

Finally we have the last group to which I personally belong. In this group, there is nothing wrong or evil or in other words sinful about a Christian being a politician, politicking and contesting elections. Firstly, because man is a political animal and that there are records of politics and elections in the Holy Bible even within nuclear families. For instance, the politics of who should lead in the family of Isaac between Esau and Jacob his brother. Even God himself was concerned in the choice of Jacob before they were born.

> *Yet before the twins were born or*
> *had done Anything good or bad in order*
> *that God's Purpose in election might*
> *stand: not by Works but by him*
> *who calls – she was told.*
> *"The older will serve the younger". Just as*
> *it is written: Jacob I loved, but*
> *Esau I hated* (Rom.9:13 NIV).

Apart from God's purpose of election as recorded, we should not lose sight of the fact that the whole world belongs to our God.

> *The earth is the Lord's and the fullness*
> *of it, the world and they who dwell in it*
> (Psalm 24:1 AV).

Well in this group, a great deal of encouragement is given to the Christians both lay and clergy to see the issue of leadership or authority as coming from God.

> *Everyone must submit himself to the governing authorities, for there is no authority except that which God has established.. The authorities that exist have been established by God.(Rom.13:1 NIV).*

It is absolutely wrong for Christians to fold their hands and watch their God-given land being taken over by the wicked, caterpillars, cankerworms and destroyers who do not have an iota of the fear of God in their heart. The Bible says that the fear of God is the beginning of wisdom. The question is: is it proper for any given family to hand over the affairs of the control of may be their father's hard earned wealth into the hand of a bad son or daughter? Can such family be handed over into the hand of wicked son? No family that is in their right mind would do that, which is allowing a criminal in their home to lead them. But I think this is acceptable in most families in the Nigerian context because rogues and thieves are made Chief, Eze or Emir in their respective homes or society. This is also the case with Christians keeping away from politics and leadership, thereby handing over the good world of their good God into the hand of the devil, Satan and his agents – wicked men.

Accordingly, it is improper and incorrect therefore for Christians to have handed over the world in which God Almighty through Christ gave them an unquestionable dominion over to the devil and his agents.

> *Indeed, we live as human beings, but we do not wage war according to human standards: for the weapons of our warfare are not merely human, but they have divine power to destroy strongholds. We destroy arguments and every proud obstacle raised up against the knowledge of God, and we take every thought captive to obey Christ (2 Corinthians 10:3-5 NRSV).*

Imagine the looting of public funds and the property of the public now belonging to just very few people. Marginalization becomes the order of the day as the minority ethnic nationalities are being sideline by the majority ethnic nationalities. Lives and properties of those from the minority groups stand the risk of being pulled down by the government's evil agents representing the wicked people who were given the opportunity of leadership in this great country of ours. And for over forty years of independence both the so-called Christians and their Moslem brothers became perpetual looters because they operated the system of government known as "kleptocracy." Apostle Paul says:

> *"What shall we say then? Shall we go on sinning so that grace may increase? By no means! We died to sin: how can we live in it any longer?"* (Rom.6.1, 2 NIV).

> ***Instead of democracy and good governance, we have "kleptocracy," dictatorship, authoritarianism and militocracy.***

Instead of democracy and good governance, we have "kleptocracy", dictatorship, authoritarianism and militocracy. These are the systems that have been militating against the proper development of this great nation – Nigeria. The backwardness we have today is a consequence or result of the people we planted in government, the selfish opportunists and mediocre. People who do not possess intellectual capability to be leaders in all ramifications. We are simply getting the reward of what was executed.

"Do not be deceived and deluded and misled: God will not allow Himself to be sneered at (scorned,

disdained, or mocked by mere pretensions or professions or by his precepts being set aside). He inevitably deludes himself who attempts to delude God. For whatever a man sows that and that only is what he will reap"(Gal.6: 7 Amplified Version).

I shall accordingly consider the tenets or ethics of Jesus Christ and St. Paul in this book by bringing what are the unethical or immoral actions, which Christian should not be partakers. This is to bring into a proper admonition of what will sound Christian or unchristian, ethical or unethical, acceptable or unacceptable according to the Christian faith.

A proper or adequate space will be given to discussing the entity called Nigeria and how she came to be. The colonial leaders and ethnic nationalities that made up the country Nigeria and the amalgamation that forced both the Northern part of the country and the southern zones to come together as one nation. The issue of indirect rule and some of the atrocities caused by the colonial masters in destroying the lives of Nigerians whenever they protested of being maltreated or under paid in their job.

The peculiar factor of Nigerian Politics shall be considered one after the other and the use of the scripture for a proper enlightenment of the reader of this book taken into consideration.

> *"Indeed, the word of God is living and active, sharper than any two edged sword, piercing until it divides soul from spirit, joints from marrow; it is able to judge the thoughts and intentions of the heart. And before him no creature is hidden, but all are naked and laid bare to the eyes of the one to whom we must render an account" (Heb.4:12,13, NRSV).*

The above scripture if considered and understood is just that it talks about the rest we should receive as Christians from the hand of God at the end of our faithful journey here on earth.

> *'Let us, therefore, make every effort to enter that rest, so that no one will fall by following their example of disobedience (Hebrew 4:112 NRSV)*

The children of Israel disobeyed God and the word of God from Moses His servant and God did not allow them to enter into the 'rest' of the Promised Land. It is also an exhortation to us to make every effort to enter into the promised rest of the second coming of Christ. It is not a call to earn one's salvation by works, but an exhortation to enter salvation rest by faith and not for their works nor to follow Israel's sad example in the desert. We know that God destroyed all those in the disobeying generation of Moses in the desert except Joshua and Caleb.

From ethnicity or ethnic syndrome to military coups, money politics, squandamania, greed, the evil roles of some traditional rulers and a lot of other problems or factors of Nigerian politics are considered. I want you to note this word of God as you delve into this book in your hand.

> "*I treasure your word in my heart, so that I may not sin against you.*"
> *(Psalm 119:11 NRSV)*

If we put the word of God in our hearts, it will be very difficult for us to fall into sin unless we so wish to fall into it. And the Psalmist also made it clear that the word of God is a lamp unto our feet.

> "*Your word is lamp to my feet and a light to my path*" *(Psalm 119:105 NRSV).*

Having a lamp and a light on our path shall guide us on our ways and we shall not stumble and fall but if the lamp and light is not there we are bound to stumble and fall flat. We know that it is hard for one to walk in darkness where there is no light. So the word of God is a lamp and light to the Christian. It is also the word of God that is the sword of the spirit.

> ***Without God leading you as a leader, you may leave office as a cursed person even with your wealth than being blessed***

This book should be interesting to those who may want to know more about God's mind with regards to politics, leadership and authority and how these could be used for all to benefit in. Remember, "power corrupts and absolute power corrupts absolutely:" Without God leading you as a leader, you may leave office as a cursed person even with your wealth than being a blessed man.

CHAPTER TWO

If we claim to have fellowship with him yet We walk in darkness, we lie and do not live by the truth. But if we walk in the light, and he is in the light we have fellowship with one another and the blood of Jesus, His Son purifies us from all sin. (I John 1:6,7 NIV).

WHO IS A CHRISTIAN?

The word 'Christian' though first coined and applied to the followers of Christ in Antioch, was then and is till date used in describing those who follow and practice the way of life of Jesus Christ. It is more likely that those who used this word on the followers of Christ were the Antiochenes pagans. It is imperative to note that the word occurs in just three places in the Bible: Acts 11:26; 26:28 and I Peter 4:16. In the above passages, it is simply used for the followers of Jesus Christ.

However, the word 'Christian' connotes different meaning and application to different groups of Christians.

While the fundamentalists Christians take the scripture literarily, the 'extremists' feel they should separate themselves from all human affairs like being involved in public affairs which they regard as sin, and there is also the liberal group who can otherwise be seen as easy going, who merged all above together but take the middle of the road.

Nevertheless, I understand the word Christian to mean one who realizes that he was separated from the Almighty God his creator by indulging in sin of all sorts and asking for forgiveness by repentance through Jesus Christ. With penitent heart he turned from his evil ways back to God his maker. Christian is the one that loves God and his neighbour and whatever is good and honourable. He or she tries to follow peace with all men and does not see salvation as coming from any other avenue than Christ. To be a Christian, one must be born again.

> *"Jesus answered him, I assure you, most solemnly I tell you, that unless a person is born again (anew from above), he cannot ever see (know, be acquainted with, and*

experience) the Kingdom of God."
(John 3:3 AV).

John the beloved Apostle of Christ also in the first chapter of this gospel said the following about the believers:

> *"But to all who receive Him, who believed in His name he gave them power to become children of God"*
> (John 1:12(b) RSV).

The above passage of the scripture does not imply that whoever received him and believed in his name is above temptation and sin and thereby making one to project, "a holier than thou" attitude. The basis of salvation is not something one can claim by works but it is simply by grace through faith. Grace is an unmerited favour from God and not something gotten because of anything of our own. It is clearly stated in the scripture that:

> *"If we say we have no sin, we deceive ourselves, and the truth is not in us. If we confess our sins, he is faithful and just, and will forgive our sins and cleanse us from all unrighteousness."*
> (I John 1:8,9 RSV).

I do not see the above as an encouragement for Christians to sin but that one should not run away from the faith because he has fallen into temptation or committed sin.

Accordingly, a Christian signifies the follower of Christ with an absolute surrendering of his or her life to the will of God and Christ's teaching. It is a call and not by might or power lest any one should boast. And to be a true Christian is to do the will of God. It is obvious Biblically that whoever sins is of the devil, and the devil or Satan is a perpetual sinner.

ETHICS AND MORALITY

Ethics comes from the Greek word ethos, meaning character or conduct and custom. Morality comes from the Latin word '*moralis*' meaning customs or manners. In other words, the two words ethics and morality are used frequently, at times one for the other. While ethics is mostly used when it pertains to business and professions, morality has to do with sexuality. For example, that lawyer's attitude was unethical while the musician is an immoral man. Commonly speaking, the two words are not very often used as we use good and bad, right and wrong. Ethics, therefore, seems to pertain to the individual character of a person or persons, whereas morality seems to point to the relationship among human beings.

Whether we call a person ethical or moral or an act unethical or immoral does not really make any difference. When we speak of a person as moral or ethical, we usually mean he or she is a good person, and when we speak of him or her as immoral or unethical, we mean that he or she is a bad person, when we refer to certain human actions as moral, ethical, immoral or unethical, we mean they are right or wrong. However, the important thing to remember here is that moral, ethical, immoral, unethical essentially mean good, right, bad, wrong, often depending on whether one is referring to people themselves or to their actions.

In summary therefore, Christian Ethics or morality may be defined as a systematic explanation of the moral example and teaching of Jesus Christ applied to the "total' life of the individual in society and actualized by the power of the Holy Spirit. It could also be called Biblical Ethics, which is concerned with the manner of life, which the Bible prescribes and approves. The ethics, which the Bible requires, is concerned with the heart of man. "For out of it are the issues of life." And "as a man thinketh in his heart so is he". The heart conceals every intentions of man, which makes him unique or peculiar in his attitude towards fellow man. That is why the Bible says, "The heart is deceitful above all things and beyond cure, who can understand it?" As you are reading this book, think it out whether you really understand the man that is very close to you or even your wife or husband. Do you understand man?

That is the reason why the act of deceitfulness - political deceitfulness during electioneering campaigns and in manifestoes is always secret to the individual or group of politicians except when an action is taken. Man is deceitful, beyond cure or healing, desperately

> ***It is only God, the creator of man that knows men's Intentions and plans in the present and future***

wicked above all and therefore who can know man? It is only God, the creator of man that knows man's intentions and plans in the present and future. The heart therefore controls the ethical or moral life of man and no man can act above what he thinks for better or for worst, moral or immoral, ethical or unethical. Most politicians, including Christians so called, are always on the negative side of whatever is ethical or moral.

CHRISTIAN BIBLICAL ETHICS

Writers dealing with the subject define Christian ethics in a variety of ways. For instance, L. S. Keyser, American Lutheran scholar, defines this discipline as "the science, which treats the sources, principles and practices of right and wrong in the light of the Holy Scriptures in addition to the right of reason and nature." This is to say that ethics involves the source or origin of the basic wrong as stated in the Bible. Emile Branner says that ethics is "the science of human conduct as it is determined by divine conduct." But for a Christian to have a divine conduct he must understand his Bible in the light of the Holy Spirit. Again Georgia Harkness, American

Methodist Theologian puts it this way, that Christian ethics is "a systematic study of the way of life exemplified and taught by Jesus, applied to the manifold problems and decisions of human existence." It all means following the example as laid down by Jesus Christ during his earthly ministry through his teachings and sermons.

Christian ethics is "a systematic study of the way of life exemplified and taught by Jesus, applied to the manifold problems and decisions of human existence."

On the other hand Biblical ethics is concerned with the manner of life, which the Bible prescribes and approves. According to the scripture, however, conducts or manners can never be disassociated from the dispositional complex, which comes to expression in observable behaviour. The ethics which the Bible requires is concerned with the heart of man, for "out of it are the issues of life," and as a man thinketh in his heart, so is he. But the dynamic of the Biblical ethics is the Holy Spirit or the Spirit of Christ. The newness of life after the pattern of Christ through his resurrection is the newness of the believers' spirit. The Holy

Spirit leads the sons of God and their virtues are fruits of the spirit and they walk by the spirit and their love, which is the fulfillment of the law, is the love of the spirit.

Furthermore, no reactions affect ethical behaviour more deeply than the fear of God. The commandment to love the Lord with all the heart and soul and mind is the first and great commandment. This fear of God is the soul of godliness, and consists in the profound apprehension of His majesty and His good pleasure is our paramount concern.

The fact of the matter is that love is paramount and must be informed by the truth, and the fear of God is the beginning of knowledge and wisdom. Faith is the fountain of ethics, love to God and neighbour the impelling motive, the law of God is the directing principle and the glory of God the governing aim. Should Christians exhibit these in their political behaviour and leadership, Nigeria would have been a better society at this point in time or in the new millennium.

POLITICS IN THE CHURCH

Is there politics in the Church? The answer to the above question is in affirmative, `yes'. Denying the fact that there is `politics' in the church is fallacious

Denying the fact that there is `politics' in the church is fallacious

or it may be that is to say on the other hand that whoever denies that there is no such thing in the church is saying so in ignorance. By `church' here I am referring to the Christians who are saved and belong to different groups of worship or denominations. In other words I am referring to the `church of Christ' through out the universe. On further explanation, the word `church' came from the Greek word "Kuriakon" meaning "belonging to the Lord." In the New Testament it is from the Greek word "Ecclesia" which means `the Christian community or congregations of Christians." So by the word church in the context in which I am using it, I am referring to the `church of Christ' – denominations whatever the name may be notwithstanding.

Do the churches have ideals or goals?
How do they pursue them? Are there leaders in the church? How are they appointed or elected? In answering the above questions one will discover that if the answers are 'yes', then the way in which the above are done cannot be exclusive of the word 'politics' which has to do with acquisition of power to pursue a particular goal or ideals. Church leaders or heads have within their church the pastors whom they love dearly and those whom they think are working for their good or interest. They also have pastors whom they do not want to hear anything good about and this set of pastors are always having it rough and rude from the leaders. The point I am making is that if you do not as a subordinate have the good deal with your may be – bishop, president, superintendent or senior pastor of your particular denomination, you must have it tough. At times, the politics of the church does not exist in the midst of ministers alone but most comes from the lay members.

The point I am making is that if you do not as a subordinate have the good deal with your may be – bishop, president, superintendent or senior pastor of your particular denomination, you must have it tough

There was an instance in which as a young minister newly commissioned and posted to my first station I had it tough because a politician who did not give a damn to the church hierarchy was the circuit steward or the second in command as misconceived or designed by those ministers who are not interested in preaching salvation messages but the praise of men. Actually as somebody that married from my village, I gave the man in question a high regard but I was also cautious. When the said man knew I was not in the habit of acting on his directives hook, line and sinker he started framing me up. At a point the said man connived with the Presbyter to pay other ministers and church workers their salaries based on a fractional calculation of one third of what you brought from your section. This he said was the directive from the Diocesan Bishop but I raised an objection to receiving anything that was not formally agreed upon on any of the church meetings and other workers joined me in solidarity.

The consequences of this was that I and other workers were summoned before the Diocesan Bishop as not allowing money to be sent to the

Bishop's office. As a result the same man made some propaganda that I declared that members from his local church were idiots and he seized a present that was brought for my induction service by his local church women's fellowship. As a lot of other things followed that event at the time I had admission into the university, I was posted to a place in which I could not cope with studies in the University of Calabar. I was in the black book of both the Bishop and Diocesan Lay President, who, if not through the grace of God would have stopped my ordination. God used another Presbyter at the eleventh hour to ensure I was ordained. A minister also stopped me from entering into the ministry of the church because of petty talks from the minister's female friend.

What am I saying? The issue is that since human beings have ideals or goals which they always pursue in life, these ideals are not pursued in a vacuum but by either intimidation or stepping on the toes of others or plainly speaking by putting up

> ***Since human beings have ideals or goals which they always pursue in life, these ideals are not pursued in a vacuum but by either intimidation or stepping on the toes of others***

Some political structures or manipulations to achieve their goals or ideals. So whether it is considered negatively or positively, there is politics in a nutshell in every sphere of human life. There is the individual, group or sectional politics within the church. After all in some occasions, ministers or pastors are not allowed entrance into the parsonage because of either the weakness of such pastors or some conception or perception about such pastors.

So, whether we consider it from the point of people admitted into the ministry, posting from one station to the other, send-off and reception services, promotion from one step of hierarchy to another and in general treatments, there is politics in all spheres of human endeavour. At times, the only difference in the politics within or outside the church is that the one within the church is one in which it is not quite clear who is your opponent like the one outside the church.

Ministers do lobby for one thing or the other, there are no two ways about that and wherever there is leadership there must be power and wherever there is power there is politics because politics is the acquisition of power for a particular ideal(s).

Ministers do lobby for one thing or the other, there are no two ways about that and wherever there is leadership there must be power and wherever there is power there is politics because politics is the acquisition of power for a particular ideal(s).

Let us meditatively, with our whole heart mind and soul join in the great song written by Charles Wesley to say or sing the following:

1. A charge to keep I have,
   A God to glorify,
   A never-dying soul to save,
   And fit if for the sky.

2. To serve the present age,
My calling to fulfill;
O may it all my powers engage
To do thy Master's will!

3. Arm me with jealous care,
As in thy sight to live;
And O Thy servant, Lord, prepare
A strict account to give.

4. Help me to watch and pray,
And on Thyself rely,
Assured, if I my trust betray,
I shall forever die.

CHRIST AND POLITICS

He is the image of the invisible God, The first born over all creation. For by him all things were created; things in heaven and on earth, visible and invisible whether thrones or powers or rulers or authorities; all things were created by him and for him. He is before all things and in him all things hold together.
(Colossians 1: 15-17 NIV)

Christ is the principal actor, the leading distributor and the absolute authority and power of all creation because God Almighty made him so.

A careful consideration of the above text has a lot to teach both Christians and non-Christians that since no man can see God, Christ is the image of the unseen – radiance of God's glory and the exact representation of his being. All things and everything, all creations – thrones or powers, rulers or authorities were all created by him and for – Christ Jesus our Lord. There is no way as a matter of fact in which the master designer, master architect, master builder, master organiser, master physician, master healer, master governor and president, master instructor, you can go on and name them, can be kept out of the order he created and then we still have the best life could offer on this planet earth. It can never be possible because all things were created by him for himself – period.

According to the word of John Howard Yoder;

> *"Society and history, even nature would be impossible without regularity system order, and this need God provided for. The*

universe is not sustained arbitrarily, immediately, and erratically by an unbroken succession of new divine interventions. It was made in an ordered form and "it was good." The creative power worked in a mediated form, by means of the Powers that regularized all visible reality."

The planet earth or the world simply would have altogether been chaotic if there was no order, even the order of having day and night, months and years. Nothing would have existed in compliance and good relationship with one another. There should be no juxtaposition on the matter of order or politics with God and Jesus Christ his son. Most Christians" impression that God is not concerned about earthly politics or political affairs – human relationship, conduct of public affairs and ideals would portray God as one who is not concerned in any way with what is happening around the creatures He created in his own image. Angels and even the Holy Spirit were not also given the power to multiply and conquer the world but God gave man that power and position in his created order to do so.

On the other hand, the ministry of Jesus

Christ though short-lived was not the type that actually gave him and his followers the time to sit down and think on how they should be involved in some social and political issues of his time. Being God-man but born into the family of a poor carpenter and also being a carpenter himself could altogether be parked into one – humility that culminated in giving out even his body to be crucified on the cross. Were not also his disciples people of the same group? Even at that time of human development, fishermen were not good materials for leadership in the social and political circles. This was the reason people marveled most times during their ministry as they spoke as men with authority especially after the Pentecost experience of the outpouring of the Holy Spirit.

What then can we say was the position of Jesus Christ or pronouncements that we can at this age and in all ages used as we go about interacting with other human beings? It is completely out of place that Jesus did not say anything in relationship to human conducts, which could be useful in the public matters. Were all his pronouncements, sermons, —

teachings only religious matters that has no relationship with socio-political matters and affairs? John Howard Yoder is of the opinion that Jesus Christ interacted on human relationship and affairs and therefore pointed out the following pronouncements of Jesus as 'The Politics of Jesus':

> "Love your enemies, do godd to those who hate you; bless those who curse you and pray for those who maltreat you."
>
> "Give to all who beg from you"

"Do to others what you would have them do to you." Be compassionate, as your father is compassionate." The above scriptures can then be divided into four and be taken one after the other.

LOVE YOUR ENEMIES, DO GOOD TO THOSE WHO HATE YOU; BLESS THOSE WHO CURSE YOU AND PRAY FOR THOSE WHO MALTREAT YOU.

(Luke 6: 27, 28)

Within the political arena, many friends and enemies are made and this has to do with the heart of man that is full of evil and wickedness. Some best political associates most of the time turn out to be worse enemies and in most cases battle lines are drawn. Many instances on this can be quoted all over the world and in our country Nigeria.

But the greatest teacher and professor that ever lived – Jesus Christ says - *'Love your enemies.'* This was the heart of his teaching - *'Love.'* Love is the essence of the character of God himself because God is LOVE – period. Though not Christians, what on earth can the family of Chief M. K. O. Abiola do in revenge to the family of Gen. I. B. Babangida and Gen. S. Abacha that can bring back a suitable father – M. K. O. Abiola and a lovely mother Kudirat Abiola? Good friends the trios were before June 12, 1993 election – but terrible enemies because the heart of man is deceitful and wicked above all things. It is only God who knows man. But Christ says, in his admonition "*Do good to those who hate you*" Is not that very difficult for one to do? Could Evan Enwerem have voted for Chuba Okadigbo to continue as the Senate President when he knew Okadigbo was too much on him that resulted in his leaving the seat of the Senate President? Today, is it not a man that was never thought of at any time to be on the seat that is now the President? Somebody said it is a "*Turn by Turn Senate President Nigeria Limited.*" We should try our best to do good to those who hate us.

With all the curses, indictment, scandals and defamation of character, we should do good and bless those who curse us. It does not stop at doing good for them but we should bless and pray for their well being. Those who are maltreating us must be considered also in our prayers.

Are you not among those Christians who would falsify election results of some candidates who actually won the election because you think they have no one to confront you or that they are not in your good book or favour? You would not allow the will of God to take its proper course and place within the affairs of men and when you thwart the will and plan of God on anybody's life in due time you shall receive your reward. Do you hear that? God is no respecter of any man or person.

Christ second position is this:

"*GIVE TO ALL WHO BEG FROM YOU*"

In whatever form or way we want to put it, we have the difficulty of giving and most of the time when the going is good so that people will leave with impression that we do not have. Think about Jesus Christ who gave himself to us as a ransom of our sins. He died on our behalf or place.

This we did not beg him to do neither did he campaign for it. Dear Christian, politician and office holder, we cannot live beyond what comes out of our mouth whether for good or bad. What we confess each day and moment is what we are going to end up with. Listen to me; what you say you are is what you surely will end up to be – sooner or later.

Most people do not give to those who beg from them even when they are in charge or control of millions of naira sent to them every month, which does not belong to them. Simply, the confessions of most of these men are: things are very difficult. I do not have a mite even here and in my account. Condition is very tough with me. I do not know how to meet up with my responsibilities. Those who beg from them after pouring out their hearts to them will go back disappointed.

When the members of the Upper Legislative House in Nigeria were sworn in sometime in June 1999 they forgot the people, their electoral pledges and the impoverish condition of most Nigerians who are living below the world poverty line by asking for extravagant furniture allowance of ₦5 million for Senators and ₦3.2 million for House of Representatives. Brothers and sisters, be reminded that "No Conditions is Permanent" and a man's life is not in the financial euphoria of his bank account and overseas trips, expensive furniture and homes, flashy cars and dresses but on the impact he made on his fellow men or mankind. Some communities have been begging for ordinary thing like bore-hole water or pipe borne water and electricity but never considered at all by those in authority.

Let me give you the analogy of one respectable Barrister I know about election or appointment into public offices or about public officers. According to Barr. Umoekoyo Uno using example of the Local Government Council:

> "That the council is like a pea fruit tree that was planted by an ancestor or forebear of a particular people. In the mind of this great father was the

notion that his family will expand and that the pea would then have been a very big tree.

As a matter of fact smaller families making up the larger one would be assigned to pluck the fruit of the tree from time to time. This does not mean that it is the family whose responsibility or turn is to climb and pluck should only benefit and it should not be the man climbing who should eat alone. The man supposing to be climbing is the Chairmen, Governors and other elected officers. You would do better if you pluck the pea and put some in your pocket while some are thrown to the aged who may be returning from the farm asking for a little. You would have saved your neck and life by giving to them out of which some will be picked up by children who are also expecting to pick up fallen crumbs will pick some up. The aged will bless you when after cooking the cassava will remember your pea to eat the said

> cassava but curses will come when you did not offer them anything. What will take place would be that of the people whom you refused their inheritance using all means to destroy all that were theirs, which you used your position to usurp. They must make sure that whatever you kept in your bag that which was in your mouth and that which was in your stomach were perfectly drained out of you and your later position will be worst than the former."

Whenever I remember this great saying and take account of former Council Chairmen I have known so far in my life and even those in other public offices, I would say to myself, what a man should rather fight for should not be acquisition of wealth but should be in contributions made in the society and to people around him. That is touching the lives of people who may in turn support you when the going is tough. It is not only that, God himself shall be your supporter. Remember, when you 'GIVE' it shall be 'GIVEN' to you until it overflows. What you offer is what you get. Give to people who beg from you and do not store up what you should be using to help others in need.

"DO TO OTHERS WHAT YOU WOULD HAVE THEM DO TO YOU".

Most of the time if not always we treat our fellow human beings in a way in which we would not like ourselves to be treated. We shatter the hopes and aspirations of so many people as we go about out day-to-day activities and businesses. We stepped on a lot of people's toes because we are financially rich or have the goodness of life because of our position. We treat people with contempt even those we may have known – brothers and sisters.

Christ is saying that as you play your game and live your day to day life, you should do to others what you would have them do to you. Politics is a game that is full of revenge and that of paying people back in the same coin. It is what has resulted in the death of too many people because they criticized or do not accept other people's view point or way of administration. If you have not criticized anybody before, if you have not supported somebody and you were not killed for it before, if you have not experienced hardship in your life before, do to others what you want them or others to do to you.

"BE COMPASSIONATE AS YOUR FATHER IS COMPASSIONATE."

The word compassion is used to translate the Hebrew word *hamal* and rah min which however stands for 'pity' or 'spare' and 'mercy' respectively, (the OT translation). In the New Testament it is *eleeo*-which translated means to 'have mercy' and have 'pity.' Through the teaching of our Lord Jesus Christ, especially in the parable of the Good Samaritan, it is clear that compassion is to be shown by his disciples to anyone who needs their help. It should be like His, not only in being without respect of persons, but also in that it is expressed in deeds (I John 3:17).

Have pity, have mercy, have a sparing spirit towards your enemies. Listen very carefully to that again, you should have a concern for other people's problem and trouble, do not be concerned for what is yours only – self first. Make some personal sacrifices, deny yourself of certain comforts and God will replenish your barn and storehouse. Store up for yourself riches in heaven and not on earth. Most politicians are not compassionate at all, they hire assassins, secret cults boys and touts to make trouble to pave way for them to win elections.

I know a so called born again Christian who did that in order to rig and win but God failed him. Jesus wants you to be compassionate to others.

IT IS NOT EASY

I want to encourage my brethren Christians that nothing good could be achieved overnight. just like becoming a preacher, medical doctor, a lawyer, engineer of all sorts, a great businessman or woman, to mention but a few, it can never be easy for a good man – a man with vision to get it easily. If you can consider what Dr. Nelson Mandela of South Africa went through because of his vision for the liberation of his kinsmen and even Olusegun Obasanjo because of few utterances against the Sani Abacha regime, you will be in a better position to know that it may be rough before you can lead your people to the Promised Land. Nelson Mandela was jailed for over a period of 27 years but came and won election that liberated his people. What he personally suffered, their children and grand children would enjoy in future. Rome it is always said was 'not built in a day' and for your political vision to materialize, it needs some times.

For your dream about the well being of your people to come to reality, it needs sometime and some processes. Ken Gaub in his book "Dreams, Plans, Goals," says that

> Many of the greatest accomplishments in history have been done against impossible odds because someone had a dream.

No one can think of being something without really giving his time to it. As Christians we need to organize ourselves, prepare our roads or ground – so they say, if we want to contribute politically to change the future of our people. Apart from great inventions which people have made which we are enjoying today, which was not an easy road, some people in the like of Abraham Lincoln who made a great name in the United States of America never had it easy. Look at the breakdown of his experience and ladder that took him to the White House and gave him the power of executing his dreams. Though he had many failures he had dream and determination to pursue it.

1831 -	He failed in business
1832 -	He was defeated for the legislature
1833 -	He failed in business again
1836 -	He had a nervous breakdown
1838 -	He was defeated for house speaker
1840 -	He was defeated for the elector
1843 -	He was defeated for congress
1855 -	He was defeated for Senate
1858 -	He was defeated for the Vice Presidency.

But in 1860 Abraham Lincoln became the sixteenth president of the United States of America because he refused to give up.

This Abraham used the word of a Baptist preacher "You can do it with God" to stir his nation with his speech on Union and slavery and contributed in stopping the obnoxious trade.

According to Rev. Robert Schuller, Tough times never last, but tough people do'. If you have a vision for this country as long as the Lord tarries and if you want it to be a reality, you need a friend and a councilor that is above every friend, and that friend is Jesus Christ, the unmoved mover or unchangeable changer."

If this book is in your hand, I want you to note that you have a destiny and purpose to wish you were created and if yours is that of creating a better environment and development to your people with all the resources in world that belongs to God, you can do it, if you will simply make up your mind to do so. To have the possibility attitude of changing what is not the best for the best, you must note according to Robert Schuller that "You would not win if you do not begin. There is no hope of winning if you do not decide to play the game." I want to personally challenge you to begin something even in your Local Government Area with men of vision and better future for the people and not naïve and visionless people who would only encourage you to loot other people's treasury, which is government money – money for your Local people,including yourself.

Some of us have the vision of having a house in Abuja, some in Lágos and other cities and most would want to own one in overseas, but the truth is that, if few wealthy men we have in the Local Government Areas within Nigeria will sit together and plan for a better place for their people, a remotest Local Government Area could become a city.

After all is not the siting of factories and other infrastructural development that makes a place a city. As you and I think in our heart, so it shall be. If you change your heart for your people you can change their environment and condition. Being in Government gives one the power to contribute immensely in making some vital policy decision and statement whose outputs could turn the life of the people around. Remember we cannot all be preachers and soul-winners – in Christ there is division of labour

Let me tell you the reader of this book, there is never a shortage of any kind with God. Thomas Edison who invented electric light said that even though he tried for 700 times to invent the light, he never saw it as a failure. When he was asked how he felt the 700 times, his answer was:

> "I have not failed, not even once. However, I have proven that 700 different ways would not work. When I eliminate all the other ways that would not work, I will find the way that works"..

The man made his dream after several hundreds of trials. Think about what life will look like if there was no electricity.

All the equipments people of this generation are today enjoying are hard work of Thomas Edison. What political decision and contribution would you make to change the lives of your people?

When people aspire to be preachers they are encouraged, when they want to read medicine both the government and parents encouraged them, when people want to be lawyers, they are persuaded to do that, even now when people want to put in their time into sports or a particular game like football they are encouraged but when people – good people desire a political office they are dissuaded. Why? Let go whatever has been keeping you from making immense contribution into building your society and move into it. Your decision today will make the life of the preacher, the doctor, the lawyer, the sportsman and woman a better one.

I am deeply persuaded and convinced that politics is not bad in the essence to which Christians have been considering it. Who gets what and how? Sharing of allocations. If you are not there your people are not recognized but your presence can change their condition. Do you believe that? You that good man, go out and the evil man will not stand your presence. Light and darkness cannot be in the same place at the same time. You can change the welfare of your people. You can have compassion on them. No more will you use English to answer them when the greet you or communicate with you in vernacular. You shall see them as your kinsmen and women, you will put yourself in their shoes and see the plights of life they are passing through, you will definitely look for a way to lessen their burden. What concerns them shall be a matter of concern to you. You will want them to see your face and not be hiding behind a dark-tinted glass of your official car. You will be a man of honour and respect before your kinsmen and women. No one shall say evil against you though some may want to discredit you because you did not adhere to their instruction of looting the Local people's fund – the Local Government 'MONEY." Pastors and Ministers, please for the sake of the Lord advise your members – Christians not rogues to be involved in planning good governance for the people. And let me tell you politicians, do not mind your pastor who will never tell you the truth of the scripture because you used to make great donations in the church – they appoint you 'knight' this or that or 'order' this or that as the case may be, your acceptability and goodness should not only be seen by your pastor alone. What of the general public?

If you have the urge to change the life of your people besides other things I think involvement in taking decisions about their welfare is important. Jesus Christ shall not in any way send you to everlasting fire because you contributed to the improvement of the life of your people. As you read this book I want you to think of ways in which the condition of your community or society could be changed through you. Remember to whom much is given will much be required. I do not only advocate that Christians should be involved in the act of leadership and politics now in Nigeria – 21st Century Nigeria but radical Christians should be involved – men of holiness gospel and not men of nobody can do `good.'

Your involvement will bring the life of a good future and hope to your people., Great men with great wisdom and power, design the type of society you want for your people now and you shall not regret. Let it not be only your children that you want to have the best in life, after all if you plan for them alone remember if they stay in overseas they are regarded as inferior people. Life is meaningless to me if we do not leave our foot-print on the sand of time. Just meditate on the words of this hymn before you read on:

1. Rise up, o men of God!
Have done with lesser things;
Give heart and soul and mind and strength
To serve the King of Kings.

2. Rise up, O men of God!
His kingdom tarries long;
Bring in the day of brotherhood,
And end the night of wrong.

3. Rise up, O men of God!
The Church for you doth wait,
Her strength unequal to her task:
Rise up and make her great.

4. Light high the cross of Christ!
Tread where this feet have trod;
As brothers of the Son of Man
Rise up, O men of God!

William Pierson Merrill 1867-

CHAPTER THREE

"Righteousness exalts a nation, but sin
is a disgrace to any people."
Prov.14: 34 NIV

NIGERIA AS A NATION

Can the above be said to be true of Nigeria? The term 'Nigeria' was invented in 1897 by Miss Flora Shaw, the Lagos correspondent of the London Times, who later became the wife of Nigeria's first Governor-General, Sir Frederick (later) Lord Lugard.

A review of history shows that Nigeria came into being in the early part of the 20th century as a legacy of British Colonial rule in Africa. That the present day state of Nigeria has been inhabited since 700 B.C. It is a land of many nations, languages, religions and cultures. And it is also interesting to note that before colonialism, these Negroid' peoples lived in separate and distinct socio-political settings. Each of the estimated 250 nations of Nigeria occupies a geographically – defined space, has its distinct language, culture and religion. The nations actually are older than the country whose name they bear.

Nigeria precisely is a country with over 800 dialects.

The three largest ethnic groups or nations are the Hausa/Fulani, Yoruba and Igbo. Nigerian population; is estimated to be about 108 million, though her census has never been properly conducted without being inflated for some political/economic reasons. The smaller nations otherwise called minorities include Edo, Kanuri, Urhobo, Tiv, Ijaw, Ogoni, Ibibio, Annang, Oro, Kalabari, Idoma and Itsekiri. Others are Ogoja, Efik, Mambila and Nupe to mention but a few. It is believed that in population, Nigeria is bigger than all the West African states put together.

The British ruled Nigeria for exactly 60 years – 1900-1960 when she was granted independence. Nigeria is also kept together by force since that time, because some nations are not willing up till date to be a part of the nation until certain issues are rectified. Between 1900 and 1914, Britain administered the different nations of Nigeria as separate protectorates, namely the Northern Protectorate and the Southern Protectorate until the final amalgamation in 1914.

> ***Nigeria is also kept together by force since that time, because some nations are not willing up till date to be a part of the nation until certain issues are ratified***

Religiously, the advent of Islam came into Hausa, Bornu and Fulani States around 14th and 15th centuries. This is why the religion is a dominant religion in Northern Nigeria, a religion considered to be a way of life by the people and even a system of government in the North. This religion has contributed in creating a major fault lines for the country of Nigeria that came into being much later.

However, Islam originally co-existed in a syncretic manner with the traditional religions of the Hausa, Fulani and Bornu States. Within 1804 and 1810, Hausa States were completely conquered by Islam, which sought conversion from personal faith to communal-Sharia. The conquering Fulani then constituted the core of the ruling classes except in Abuja and Daura States of Hausa land. The kingdom of Borno, home of the Kanuri however successfully resisted incorporation into the Fulani Empire.

On the other hand, the half-century before 1891 marked a period of robust and sustained Christian missionary activity in Southern Nigeria which has left an indelible mark on the nations of that part of Nigeria. The inception of a new dawn of missionary activities was 1841 in which the first British expedition up on Africa great waterways, River Niger, was made. It was also in 1891 that the great Bishop, Legendary Ajayi Crowther died.

Monarchs of the Nations of Southern Nigeria were participating in the sale of fellow Africans to

Another great thing but disastrous issue that also took place in the 19th century was the Trans-Atlantic slave trade which was very much in full swing before the middle of the century. Monarchs of the Nations of Southern Nigeria were participating in the sale of fellow Africans to Europeans. Nations in Southern Nigeria were so much affected by the slave trade as millions of our people passed through door of no return on Gores Island in Senegal to the New World – North America, South America and Cuba.

Consequently, the activities of the Christian Missions of 19th century focused on the need to bring an end to the slave trade and attacking it at its African source. According to Buxton, a leading British Evangelical Missionary,

> "*Elevating the minds of her people and calling forth, the resources of her soil... let missionaries and school masters, the plow and spade, go together and agriculture will flourish, the avenues of legitimate commerce will be opened, confidence between man and man will be inspired, while civil- -ization will advance and Christianity operate as the proximate cause of this happy change.*"

In fact, church and school came hand-in-glove to the nations of Southern Nigeria during that era of Christian missionary activities. All the city-states and nations within Southern Nigeria requested for schools to teach their children in welcoming the Christian missions. This exposure to Western Education laid the foundation for a tremendous intellectual development in

> ***This exposure to Western Education laid the foundation for a tremendous intellectual development in Southern part of Nigeria, compared to the very slow development of those in the North***

Southern part of Nigeria, compared to the very slow development of those in the North.

This created a great gap which was later widened into an Educational fault line by the policy of the British colonial government which discouraged Christianity in the North because of the obnoxious activities in the Muslim emirates of Northern Nigeria.

The end of the Second World War was a remarkable time in the governance of Nigeria with the introduction of parliamentary forms of government. Before that time, Lugard had introduced the system of indirect rule where monarchs were used to represent British authority in the provinces. But in the South Eastern, Lugard appointed Warrant chiefs because the people were running and operating sedentary system of government. For a more cohesive British rule, North and South were amalgamated on 1 January 1914 and Lugard was appointed the new nation's governor general.

It was not a smooth affair altogether as opposition and rebellion started gaining momentum against the British Rule in the 20th century. There was the Satiru Revolt organized by Mahdists to protest the overthrow of the Sokoto Caliphate in 1906. This was violently crushed by the British. Lives and properties were destroyed. There were other rebellions like the Ijemo in Abeokuta in 1918, Iseyin in 1916 and also women riots of 1929. There was also the first general strike in Nigeria led by Michael Imodu with railway workers in 1945. This was caused by the refusal of the British government to accept the workers' demand for an increase of 50 percent in salary. In 1949, there was the miners' strike in Enugu over improved working conditions. The British ordered soldiers to shoot at sight the protesting miners. Nigerians later adopted this style on fellow Nigerians e.g. President Obasanjo's government and the people of Odi in Bayelsa and OPC in Ketu – Lagos. Though not on the issue of strike as the case was in 1949.

Between 1900 to 1960 their colonial masters – the British government, forced series of constitutions on Nigerians through their representatives like Lord Lugard, Sir Hugh Clifford did just that and in response a Nigerian of high repute, a nationalist, a man who formed the first political party, Herbert Macaulay, a surveyor by profession attacked vigorously. His party, Nigerian National Democratic Party was formed in 1923. After Clifford's was the Arthur Richards' Constitution of 1944, while that of Sir John Macpherson came up in 1951. There was also the Oliver Lyttleton Constitution of 1954 which marked the beginning of Federal system of government in Nigeria. But earlier in 1953 a Member of Parliament Chief Anthony Enahoro had stunned the British by moving a motion that Nigeria should be self-governing by 1956.

Accordingly, in 1957, a constitutional conference was held in London from May 23 to June 26 under the Chairmanship of Allan Lennox-Boyd who made way for the internal government for the Western and Eastern regions of Nigeria. The North was to achieve the same status in 1959 –

But earlier in 1953 a Member of Parliament Chief Anthony Enahoro had stunned the British by moving a motion that Nigeria should be self-

two years after the South. On October 1, 1960 Nigeria became an independent nation with Tafawa Balewa as the first Prime Minister and Nnamdi Azikiwe as the first Governor-General.

In 1956, oil was first discovered in commercial quantity at Oloibiri – in what later became Rivers State. The Anglo Dutch Company Shell D'arcy first exported it in 1958. It is considered today that Nigeria is the 6th largest producer of Crude Oil in the world but is listed among the poorest countries of the world because of the obnoxious activities of those who have one way or the other been in charge or in authority from 1960 till date – 2000.

Prominent Nigerians, from Chief Obafemi Awolowo, Alhaji Tafawa Balewa, Major General Aguiyi-Ironsi, Alhaji Shehu Shagari and even a one time British Governor General in Nigeria have been quoted by Senator Chuba Okadigbo as backing the fact that "Nigeria since the amalgamation of Southern and Northern Nigeria in 1914, has existed as a country only -

on paper, it is still far from being united. Nigeria's unity is only a British intention for the country."

Worse still, Nigeria is not only stratified into ethnic groups nations but into socio-economic groups of the very rich class and the very poor class.

Taking the above together, it is here affirmed that Nigeria is fundamentally a multi-ethnic, multi-religious, and multi-cultural Country, i.e. a pluralistic society per excellent forced to live together with one another. Socially and politically, Nigeria is segmented into multifarious corporate groups with

Worse still, Nigeria is not only stratified into ethnic groups nations but into socio-economic groups of the very rich class and the very poor class.

differences. Worse still, Nigeria is not only stratified into ethnic groups nations but into socio-economic groups of the very rich class and the very poor class.

Furthermore, a political scientist, Chief Arthur Nwankwo in his essay published in the News Magazine of 25th May, 1998, affirmed this by saying that:

> "*Once this artificial geo-political expression became a nation state in 1914, its different ethnic nationalities never lost sight of their historical rooting and cultural diversities in spite of colonial administrative strategies and the pan national political and ideological consciousness spawned by the anti colonialist agitator during the colonial period and thereafter. Thus the principal and most fundamental of all national social forces is the ethnic nationality factor and this demonstrated throughout the intervening post independence decades (1960-1998).*"

According to the above, and even with the

creation of 36 states and Abuja as Federal Capital Territory, and 774 Local Government Areas in order to breakdown the ethnic blocks or nationalities in the country, Nigeria is still flapping her wings in the air and unable to move forward. Nigeria, I should say, because of the ethnic nationalities is a very complex society that exists as one entity through the special grace of God Almighty with justice standing a far off especially on the national levels. Leaders do not see Nigeria as a whole as their constituency but only their ethnic nationality group and their close allies or friends.

> *Leaders do not see Nigeria as a whole as their constituency but only their ethnic nationality group and close allies or friends*

Above all, Nigeria within her 40 years of independence as a sovereign state has had twelve successive national or central governments under different or twelve leaders. Sir Abubakar Tafawa Balewa (October 1, 1960 – January 15, 1966); Major General J.T.U. Aguiyi-Ironsi (January 17, 1966 to July 29, 1966); General Yakubu Gowon (August 1, 1966 to July

29, 1975) and General Murtala Mohammed (July 30, 1975 to February 13, 1976). Others are General Olusegun Obasanjo (February 14, 1976 to October 1, 1979). Alhaji Shehu Shagari (October 1, 1979 to December 31, 1983); Major-General Muhammadu Buhari (January 1, 1984 to August 27, 1985); General Ibrahim B. Babangida (August 27, 1985 to August 26, 1993); Chief Ernest Shonekan (August 26 1993 to November 27, 1993); General Sani Abacha (November 27, 1993 to June 8, 1998); General Abdulsalami Abubakar (June 8,1998 to May 29, 1999) and Chief Matthew Olusegun Obasanjo (May 29, 1999 till date).

From all that we have so far known about Nigeria, one will definitely conclude that Nigeria as the most populous black nation exists as one entity through the mercy and grace of God Almighty. The fushion of the ethnic nationalities must be regularized on justice, and agreement and equity. The Bible says in Proverb 29:4 "By justice a king gives a country stability," and in agreement, Amos 3:3 posed this question, "Do two walk together unless they have agreed to do so"? St Paul in his letter to the Corinthians in 2 Cor.3:13 says "Our desire is not that others might be relieved while you are hard pressed, but that there might be equality," all quotes from NIV. At this juncture I can boldly say that the problems of instability in Nigeria from inception is that there has never been justice especially to the people in which the country got 80 percent of her income. Secondly, the ethnic nationalities should be called to sit together and on equal representatives to chart their existence as one nation. Lastly there must be equity, and not one ethnic nationality lording it over others with force, military might and unascertained population figures. I think that I am not wrong to join those calling on the Federal Government to constitute as a matter of urgency Sovereign National Conference. This country also should learn some lessons from history – U.S.S.R. that has broken into pieces as at when due.

Fellow Nigerians and Christians, we should use justice as a foundation in which we built Nigeria. There can never be failure and backwardness where justice reigns. The Bible says:

"But let justice roll on like a river

righteousness like a never failing stream."
(Amos 5:24 NIV).

"*When justice is done, it brings joy to the righteous, but terror to evildoers.*"
(Proverb 21:15 NIV).

CHAPTER FOUR

> *"There is no authority except from God."*
>
> (Rom. 13:1)

POLITICS

By 'Politics', I know we mean the conduct of public affairs by acting or judging wisely. According to H. M. Kuitert, he presupposes that the term politics has two components:

1. "Ideals" and
2. "Gaining power in order to realize those ideals."

That is to say that people that have ideals both in the family and in public and thereby also look for power to realize those ideals are politicians. Politics also has to do with human relationship, man's interest and take regard of what others do and many pursue share goals. The primary

> *The primary aspect of politics as I know is decision making. Politics is a social phenomenon.*

aspect of politics as I know is decision making. Politics is a social phenomenon.

Furthermore, Aristotle opines that, "the one who lives outside politics is either a beast or a god." To him therefore, man is a political animal. Accordingly, if politics is all about the conduct of public affairs, ideals and gaining of power for those ideals, it begins in a nutshell from home-nuclear family. Compare the choice of Jacob instead of his brother Esau both by God and the strategic plans by his mother to actualized his election – Genesis 25: 21-34 & Rom. 9: 10-18. Politics and man is inseparable.

It is a game which could be played in either a positive or negative way, good or bad, clean or dirty ways based on individuals or the society. That is why it must not be left for mediocres, idiots and crooks as viewed by the Christians and the public as a whole. Men of integrity and honesty who are neither parochial or myopic through their actions and attitudes, hardcore Christians, that is, the real Christians who are born again should as a matter of fact be involved and contest election into political offices.

According to Omenihu C. Nwaorgu in his book "Dimensions of Political Analysis:

> "Politics is more like a balloon and a man finds himself inside it," not more as a matter of choice but as a fact of his existence.

That is to say that whether we like it or not we must one way or the other participate in the act of politics or political affairs. Accordingly Dahl (Modern Political Analysis) says politics is:

> "an unavoidable fact of human existence, which a citizen encounters on a regular basis in his interactions within the political system, town, school, church, business, firm, trade unions and a host of other associations."

The truth is that no matter the level of your spirituality and Pentecostal experience(s) you cannot avoid the game entirely since it is part and parcel of every association and organization. That some people simply look at it from one angle as a dirty game is the reason why so many of us switched off our minds about it. But it must be there. Wherever you are. It is the notion of looking at it from one angle that may have encouraged Benn (1995) to define politics as:

> "the art of looking for trouble, finding it where it exists or not, diagnosing it wrongly, and applying the wrong remedy.":

The above definition emanates from the fact that Benn never sees anything good at all about Politics. But there are good things in politics when good men are involved. The development of a state or people cannot take place when men do not organize themselves and plan their programmes on how their environment should be designed for a better living.

I think it is necessary to also consider a definition by David Easton which could for now be regarded as standard definition as far as politics is concerned. He defined politics as:

> "authoritative allocation of values".

Omenihu Nwaorgu went on to explain the above in the following way or terms:

> "Values may be understood here among other things, as preferences.

> The distribution or allocation of these values is by and large a decision making function, which must be done by an established, rightly constituted and widely accepted authority. Without authority, and such that is clad with the conditions mentioned above, the allocation may not be widely accepted within a defined territory.

But in some other way another man Lasswell says politics is basically the question of who gets what and How? If we support you to win election or if we join the PDP, APP or AD, what can the party offer to our people? I think this is practically what is happening in the present political dispensation of the present government of President Matthew Olusegun Obasanjo, though to an extent. Key offices or position are shared to the six geo-political zones of Nigeria so that partially all the Zones may be involved in the government and decision-making. This also reflects the elements of power, authority, decision making which results in allocations of the "what, to who and by the means and processes of 'How'? as determined by the authority."

When we do not humble ourselves – (Christians) in order to get the meaning of politics into our head, there is no way the evil men would not continue to be in-charge and we (Christians) will continue to complain. Even though one said that politics is "a crazy man dance;" I want us to note that Christians involvement may make it a clean and better game. It can never be clean when clean people are not involved and never can it be good if good people of God are not in it.

I am a true believer in the righteous-ness of God through Christ Jesus and when the righteous are involved things would turn to the right side and the game clean. Choice of people would be based on merit and integrity and not on what one acquires through looting of government treasury to be rich or by the obnoxious 419 – OBT (obtaining by tricks) businesses. What do you want for your people and society? What are your visions for your people? The wonderful cities you have experienced out of your local area did not just spring up one day or night. People put their heads together and planned it and today you want to be there, what have you done to your people? What do you have to offer them? Play a good politics and turn your environment into a city if you so wish.

POLITICIAN

Politician is a person taking part in politics or much interested in politics. In a bad sense it is a person who follows politics as a career regardless of principles. In other words, a politician is one involved in the game of politics and fighting for control of public affairs through appointment or election. In essence, the game of politics is for politicians and as those who play football are called footballers, those who play politics are called politicians. Interchangeably, politicians are those who plan and map out strategies on how to gain power and or how to win elections.

The question then will be; is it right for Christians to have anything to do with politics and thereby become politicians? Is it wrong for the righteous to be involved in leading the people? Must the Christians continue to leave the world which their heavenly Father created in the hands of the wicked and unrighteous people? I can say authoritatively that a righteous man is the apple of God's eye and a man of vision. If such people are involved in politics, the people whom they govern will not perish, "...where there is no vision people perish." That is, where there is no vision the people and nation perish. The fear of the Lord brings prosperity because He cares for those who acknowledge Him as God and blesses those who do His will. He honours them in all they do. (Psalm 15:4).

MILITARY

I think it is proper to say something precisely about the military at this point. The primary aspect of politics as I know is decision making. Politics is a social phenomenon. Such people receive tactical training on how to defend or offend enemies in times of conflicts and wars. Their training does

> ***The primary aspect of politics as I know is decision making.***

not primarily have anything to do with public administration. Hence, their duty is supposed to either be in their barracks or in the battlefield. They are not politicians and are not trained in the art of politicking or democratization. Theirs is orders must be obeyed without complaint hence their gaining of power through coups which lead to dictatorship or authoritarianism, and anarchy as the case may be is intolerable. They are the army, navy and air force in the Nigerian context.

AUTHORITY AND POWER

> "*Everyone must submit himself to governing authorities, for there is no authority except that which God has established*" (Rom.13:1 NIV).

The point here is that God has ordained authority and given man the power to lead from time to time. Accordingly, Prof. N. S. S. Iwe defines authority as:

> "*the directing and unifying principles of social action for the achievement of social goals of the group. In essence it is a legitimate*

moral faculty to direct or order the actions of members of the society. Here *authority and power are interchangeable in reality*."

A further explanation of the above is that authority is a social action for achieving social goals of a group. It could be given by appointment and can also be taken away even if the power of the authority comes from God. It is not for self-aggrandizement but should be used with meekness and simplicity. It could be acquired through apprenticeship. Authority is also power to give order that must be carried out.

However, power is the ability to do or not. Broadly speaking, power simply means ability. It is also a special ability i.e. ability to make other people do what they are wanted to do. It also means using the threat of superior force as in the case of leaders like Nigerian late dictator, General Sanni Abacha during his fake transition programmes, even when people were unwilling to do so. One good example is the case of Chief Don Etiebet forced to denounce his presidential ambition and party to join another party as a floor member.

When power is used in the way mentioned above, it is abused, misdirected and misfired. That is why it is always said that "power corrupts and absolute power corrupts absolutely."

> ***Power can be given and taken a way and that is to say that power as far as man is concerned is not permanent but brief.***

Power can be given and taken a way and that is to say that power as far as man is concerned is not permanent but brief. Power is relevant when it is used judiciously and irrelevant when it is used in pursuing things of personal interest. On a local level even Local Government Area Chairmen can be singled out for abuse of power in a degree unknown before in my life. Power has been used absolutely, and abused absolutely,,

even by "born again Christians" as some presented themselves. Notwithstanding what they professed, they were actually born against Christ and against his teaching.

LEADERSHIP

A leader is one that leads and according to Prof. N.S.S. Iwe, in a sense "leadership is to a society or organization what the eye is to human person." It is indispensable of any social organization or institution. In the words of Prof. Iwe, a leader is one who.

- Gives direction and guidance
- Formulates policies and guidelines for action
- Initiates plans and programme
- Coordinates the execution and implementation of policies
- Stimulates, sustains and raises morale
- Assesses and evaluates performance
- Resolves issues and conflicts
- Is the dedicated custodian of the welfare of those under his jurisdiction or sphere of authority.

Leadership is seen in the following areas: political, ecclesiastical, cultural, educational, economic and diplomatic leadership. But the best form of leadership in any of the areas especially in the political sphere must be a transformative leadership. It should neither be the transactional leadership of the politicians nor the instantly "transcending" leadership of the soldiers in the Nigerian context. The said situation in our country is that instead of transformative leadership, we have rulers with iron fist and sledgehammer on the opposition and the press or critics of any form or kind. The word of God says in Proverbs 10:17,

"He who heeds discipline shows the way to life,

but whoever ignores correction leads others astray."

Nigerian leaders ignore corrections of any form and continue to lead the whole country astray and into economic morass. The consequences are enormous – hence Kleptocracy by few and poverty by the majority

DEMOCRACY

The word 'democracy' has varieties of meanings to different background and orientation. Like other forms of government, monarchy, aristocracy, theocracy etc democracy is also a system that has to do with the generality of the people in any given state or nation. As Prof. N.S.S. Iwe puts it:

"Democracy is the will of the majority of people

> *as the basis of governmental power. It is a direct or indirect participation of the people in functions of the government. It is the ascertainment of the will and decision and opinion of the people through referendum or plebiscite and through periodic free and fair election based on adult suffrage, the law, equality of opportunity and the ideal of social justice; the recognition of the fundamental freedoms of man especially freedom of opinion and its expression of conscience and Association and assembly."*

In the above definition of democracy, the complete expression of what democracy is all about i.e. power participation, decision, opinion, free and fair elections. It also includes respect to the rules of law, and equality of all. Other items within democracy are social justice, fundamental freedom – opinion, expression, conscience, religion, association and assembly.

That is all democratization entails. Late General Sani Abacha confirmed this in his acceptance speech of the draft constitution by the Constitutional Conference on June 27, 1995.

> *"A common denominator for all forms of democracy is the belief that power is legitimate if it flows from the authority and consent of the people."*

But the late dictator did the opposite before his demise on June 8, 1998.

> ***'Democracy' is the government of the people, by the people and for the people. It is not diarchy nor dictatorship as generally practiced in African countries and other third world nations***

To put it in a more simple form, 'Democracy' is the government of the people, by the people and for the people. It is not diarchy nor dictatorship as generally practiced in African countries and other third world nations. It is not a government by threat which I simply called "Threatocracy," it is not a "Wayocracy" – government through tricks or intrigues, it is not "selectocracy" – government where a few people connive and push somebody into office, not through the consent of the masses like most of the transition programmes and elections conducted in Nigeria by Babangida and Abacha governments or administrations. Democracy is not militocracy, which is government of the military as practiced in some States in the West African Sub Region. It is not a government where those in authority cannot be criticized by the opposition, nor is it a government where crack down on opposition and mass media – journalists – is in full force. It is not a government where sycophancy is allowed nor is it government of anarchy where tension, fear and assassination are carried out like the assassination of Pa Alfred Rewane, Alhaja Kudirat Abiola and others.

Conclusively, as stated by B. O. Nwabueze in his book "*Democratisation*"

> "*There can be no democracy truly so called unless the condition of society itself is democratic, by which is meant that it should be nearly equal among the people. Equality of condition*

implies where members, are independent of each other, none being subservient to another, as in an aristocratic society where every wealthy aristocrat constitutes the head of permanent and compulsory association, composed of all those who are dependent upon him."

So when the condition and everything in the society is allowed to take democratic shape, that is where democracy is practiced. On a very strong and unequivocal note, democracy is not Kleptocracy – government by thieves.

CHAPTER FIVE

"Where there is no vision the people perish."

NIGERIAN POLITICS – PROBLEMS

This part of the book is what tickles me so much about Nigeria as a sovereign nation or state and the way Nigerians indulge in terrible things that do not allow them to move forward and to take its proper place in the comity of nations. The Bible says in Proverb 29:12 NIV, *If a ruler listens to lies, all his officials become wicked."* This is the case within Nigerian political arena where leaders listen so much to lies and sycophancy and the consequence is the wickedness of government officials. Another interesting fact we should take note of is that which has to do with stability which has been lacking within Nigeria as a nation and some

where leaders listen so much to lies and sycophancy and the consequence is the wickedness of government officials

ethnic nationalities especially within the last decade of the 20th century. Proverbs 29:4 provides the answer to that :

"By justice a king gives a country stability" (NIV)

We have lacked justice right from independence till the present moment in history.

Apart from the above, there are so many factors militating against the growth of Nigeria as a nation and a true federation politically. These factors have contributed immensely in painting a very dirty picture of politics in Nigeria especially from the Christians perspective.

MAJOR FACTORS

ETHNICITY:

Ethnicity is defined by Okwudiba Nnoli as *"a social phenomenon associated with interactions among members of different ethnic groups.*

Ethnic groups according to him are social formations distinguished by the communal character of their boundaries. Nigeria as a nation is made up of 250 ethnic groups, with over 800 dialects. One would imagine the kind of threat these diverse groups will pose to one another. This phenomenon therefore is the most serious and fundamental problem that hangs Nigeria in the neck and also drags her backward since its amalgamation in 1914.

Everything done in this country politically, economically and religiously is done along the ethnic lines and also has the influence of ethnicity highly amplified. The Hausa/Fulani who claims to be the majority group since independence marginalized other groups including the Yorubas and Igbos who were the producers of some of the first Nigerian nationalists that fought for Nigeria's independence. When Major Kaduna Nzeogwu staged the first military coup in the history of Nigeria, he was accused of not touching any fellow from his Igbo nationality. This obsenable bias was a great mistake. Consequently, when the second coup was staged on July 29, 1966, it was to avenge the errors of the first coup that took place on January 15, 1966. And with the action of Major-General Aguiyi Ironsi declaring Nigeria as a unitary state, matters were not better. The first was led by an Igbo man in which an Hausa/Fulani man,

Everything done in this country politically, economically and religiously is done along the ethnic lines

Alhaji Abubakar Tafawa Balewa was assassinated, while the second one was carried out by the Hausa/Fulani or Northerners, since Yakubu Gowon is neither Hausa or Fulani. In their coup, Major-General Ironsi, the Head of State and an Igbo man was killed with a Yoruba Officer his host. And yet the unitary form of government was sustained till 1999.

In Akinyide Osuntokun's book `Power Broker,' a biography of Sir Kashim Ibrahim, the following declaration is credited to him, Sir Kashim:

> *Sir Kashim made it quite plain to Hassan that if Ogundipe should become Head of State, he would have powers to invite an outside power to help him, and he might use such a power against the North. He advised that since the North controlled the army, the Northern boys should stick to their guns and not relinquish national leadership to anybody outside the North no*

matter what military precedence might take.

The above was made when the revenge and second coup was staged in Nigeria by the Northerners against the Igbos: and Nigeria since that time has been under the dictate of the Hausa/Fulani hegemony until February 13, 1976 when Obasanjo became the Head of State by chance, August 1993 when Ernest Shonekan also became Head by chance and finally on May 29, 1999 when Chief Matthew Olusegun Obasanjo was sworn in as the President of the Federal Republic of Nigeria at Eagle Square, Abuja.

Accordingly, the issue of Nigeria being badly stratified and destroyed by ethnicity should be a thing of concern to all Christians within Nigeria. After all, "in Christ there is no Jew or Greek, free or bound, man or woman."

What Kashim Ibrahim said at that point in history has held Nigeria spell bound until May 1999, through the special grace of God. The Northerners did not give a damn to the consequences of such clutch to power as long as they were in charge. My question then was, "How long will God the author of all things allow them to be in charge? For even the Roman Power and other ancient powers in their due time or season collapsed and fell. Christians should rise and fight against ethnicity in order to move the country forward, after all there will be no tribe in the kingdom of God.

the issue of Nigeria being badly stratified and destroyed by ethnicity should be a thing of concern to all Christians within Nigeria

after all there will be no tribe in the kingdom of God.

After this I looked and there before me was a great multitude that no one could count from every nation, tribe, people and language, standing before the throne and in front of the lamb. They were wearing white robes and were holding palm branches in their hands... salvation... lamb. Rev. 7:9-10 (NIV).

We know that Abiola, M. K. O. was not allowed into the Aso Rock because he was a southerner of Yoruba nationality even though he was the winner of the freest and fairest election conducted in the history of Nigeria as a nation. Though this may have been a let down considering his alleged contribution during change of governments baton of power in Nigeria. After all General I. B. Babangida used Abiola's private jet when he staged a coup that ousted Gen. Muhammadu Buhari and Gen. Tunde Idiagbon from power.

> *Do not be deceived and deluded and misled God will not allow Himself to be sneered at (Scored, disdained, or mocked by mere pretensions or professions or by his precepts being set aside). (He inevitably deludes himself who attempts to delude God). For whatever a man sows, that only is what he will reap.* (Gal. 6:7 AV)

> ***Ethnicity has created hostility, imbalance, intemperate utterances, violence and socio-economic competition.***

Apart from the above, ethnicity has created hostility, imbalance, intemperate utterances, violence and socio-economic competition, which has retarded the growth of the country over the years.

RELIGIOUS PLURALISM:

Another terrible factor which is also at the peak of Nigeria's political problems, with ethnicity, is religious multiplicity practices. Though Christianity and Islam could be seen as the two major religious groups within Nigeria, besides African traditional religions. The first two religions have created an atmosphere of crises, rancour, intolerance and other vices.

Firstly, within the Christian fold, there are so much divisions that one may wonder whether Christians used one sacred book "*The Holy Bible*" as their only guide, tenet of practices and standard in all matters. Christians are so much divided among themselves that even a handful of people regard themselves as the only Group that is righteous before God. Thus the "Holier than thou concept." Some of the churches are seen, as being dead while others are spiritual and Pentecostal.

On the other hand, within the Islamic religion in Nigeria we have groups made up of Moslem radicals. They are always rioters and are used at times to fight against the Christians in the Northern Nigeria towns like Kano, Kaduna, Katsina, et cetra.

What I intend to put across is that Christians should take their rightful position in the scheme of things in the political arena of this nation. Consider this scripture:

> "*God had planned something better for us so that only together would they be made perfect*." (Heb: 11:14 NIV).

If Christians in the true sense of what Christians should be are not involved, things would not be perfected in Nigeria. For a perfect thing we need perfect group of people to be in charge.

> "*But the noble, open-hearted, and liberal man devises noble things and he stands for*

for what is noble, open-hearted and generous." (Isaiah 32:8 AV.)

Through the Prophet Jeremiah, we also are aware of the fact that God Almighty has some plans for us.

> "*For I know the plans I have for you, declares the Lord "Plans to prosper you and not to harm you, plans to give you hope and future". Then you all will call upon me and come and pray to me and I will listen to you, you will seek me and find me when you seek me with all your heart.* (Jeremiah 29:11-13 NIV)

Does God encourage us here to fold our hands and sit tight in order for his plans to be unfolded in lives and society?

Does God encourage us here to fold our hands and sit tight in order for his plans to be unfolded in lives and society? God's plans can only be achieved when we are involved in contributing our quota before it is successful. That is not to say that God cannot also work out His plans without our involvement. He is in charge but wants to use us as His instruments as He used Jesus Christ His son for the redemption of mankind.

"*The Lord will make you the head, not the tail if you pay attention to the commands of the Lord your God...*" *You will always be at the top never at the bottom.*" (Deut. 28: 13 NIV)

Furthermore, I want to say that we should not be troubled about the enactment of Sharia laws in some states at this point because God has plan for everything as He has made it known in His word:

"*And we know that in all things God works for good of those who love Him, who have been called according to His purpose.*" (Romans 8:28 NIV)

The other main issue with the Christians is that of lack of love which is seen as the base of the religion. We do not love ourselves, we do not love our neighbour and we do not see ourselves as members of one big family with God as our father and Jesus Christ as our senior/elder brother. The house that fights against itself cannot stand and this has been our major problem in Christianity.

"If I speak in the tongues of men and of angels, but have not love, I am only a resounding gong or a clanging cymbals"
(I Cor. 13:1 NIV)

We cannot support our brother whom we know as a Christian rather we go for an unbeliever because of his money power.

> ***We cannot support our brother whom we know as a Christian rather we go for an unbeliever because of his money power***

We rather ignore our Christian brother and vote simply because we got fifty naira, one hundred naira or one thousand naira from his opponents' campaign team not minding whether he has the fear of God in his life which is the beginning of wisdom.

Vast Wealth – Mineral Resources:

Nigeria is rated as the 6th largest producer of petroleum in the world which is a great blessing from God. During the regime of Gen. Yakubu Gowon, Nigeria recorded what was considered in the early 70s as oil boom and the money from which the leaders squandered extravagantly during FESTAC '77. With a lot of oil wells scattered throughout the Southern Niger Delta area of Nigeria and exposure through it, Nigerians who have access to the areas and were in charge of the minerals made their millions and billions of naira to the detriment of ordinary Nigerians. The Bible says that:

> "*The love of money is a root of all kinds of evil.*" I Tim. 6:10A

The looters also did so much of their lootings to the detriment of the oil producing areas which has resulted in a lot of crises in recent times and mostly at the close of 20th century. Those who produce the bulk of the wealth are deprived; the wealth which should make them happier is now the source of their political repression and economic deprivation. Nigerians are so much conscious of money that they at most times sold out their people's quota for money in order for us to be rich.

> ***Nigerians are so much conscious of money that they at most times sold out their people's quota for money in order for***

Nigerians are so much used

to money and want to be rich men and women as quick as possible; without money, we are not interested in anything. So that what the Bible says:

> *"Men prepare a meal for enjoyment*
> *and wine makes life new, and*
> *money is the answer to everything."*
> (Prov. 10: 19 ASV.)

The above is a fulfilled scripture in the Nigerian context. Nigerians are so addicted to money that a Nigerian can call `black', `white' so far as he got his package from it. This is a very serious problem within Nigerian politicians and Christians which has some consequences on every Nigerian. We are lovers of money and wealth at the expense of our birthright, rules of law, fundamental human rights and our privileges. It is all-detrimental to our intellectual power and spiritual foresight. Christians must come out of the circle of money lovers.

Nigerians are so addicted to money that a Nigerian can call `black', `white' so far as he got his package from it

GREED AND SELFISHNESS:

Since the oil boom of the 70s which resulted in Nigerian leaders becoming squander maniacs, corruption and indiscipline continued to proliferate Nigerian society. General Murtala Mohammed tried to transform Nigeria without knowing that in the process he had cut a deep wound in the Middle Belt sector of the military and was killed. General Muhammadu Buhari and his counterpart, General Tunde Idiagbon also tried to turn Nigeria away from indiscipline and corruption but were pushed out of office by General Ibrahim Babangida and his cohorts.

Accordingly, because there is corruption through greed and selfishness which the Bible is strictly against in high places within Nigeria, the whole country, Christians inclusive are corrupt. Chuba Okadigbo, the new millennium Senate President states this:

> 'The vicious circle goes like this, bribe the Messenger, if you may see his boss. Bribe the Clerk, if your file may move up. Bribe the Chief Clerk, if you want a form. Bribe the

executive if you want to be considered for a job or contract. Bribe the Permanent Secretary, if you may be short-listed for contracting. Bribe the minister when you get the award and pay some advance bribe before you get that contract..."

One can go on and on like that without end. A job without bribe is no job at all in Nigeria.

Every Nigerian, apart from wanting to be in oil companies, desires job offers in the Nigeria Police Force, Customs, Immigration and National Drug Law Enforcement Agency and the armed forces.

Every Nigerian, apart from wanting to be in oil companies, desires job offers in the Nigeria Police Force, Customs, Immigration and National Drug Law Enforcement Agency and the armed forces. In politics, you must begin your bribery from NECON to the SSS, to the Police, to the party officials and members before the electorate if you must be voted for. Election figures may be changed as soon as one offers a huge bribe to the electoral officers only for the loser to be declare the winner at the final analysis. Christians listen to what the Bible says about bribe:

> "*Do not accept a bribe, for a bribe blinds Those who see and twists the words Of the righteous.*" Exodus 23:8 NIV
>
> "*You shall not misinterpret or misapply judgment;; you shall not be partial, or take bribe, for a bribe blinds the eyes of the wise and perverts the words of the righteous.*"
> Deut. 15:19 AV

And in the final pronouncement of those who take bribe this is what the Bible says:

> "*Curse is he who takes bribe.*" Deut. 27:23 AV

Dear fellow Christians let this not be mentioned against us again for it shall profit a man nothing if he gains the whole world and looses his soul.

Leaders end up accumulating vast wealth for themselves, being assisted by the `Christians who are always appointed into the offices like that of minister for finance and the acquisition of the wealth is done at the

POWER-MANIA:

It is quite unfortunate that Nigeria, which should be an extra ordinary example for other African nations that are less developed, should rather emulate these small countries' bad examples of leadership. The populations of Lagos State alone are more than that of some of the countries and from one regime to another Nigerian leaders are often fond of trying to perpetuate themselves in power. This they did forgetting what they declared on their mission when they took over power through coup *d'etat.* For the love of power others termed `power mania' these leaders end up accumulating vast wealth for themselves, being assisted by the `Christians who are always appointed into the offices like that of minister for finance and the acquisition of the wealth is done at the expense of the poor masses.

Consequently, apart from Major-General Aguiyi-Ironsi and General Murtala Mohammed who stayed just six months in office before meeting their death, and General Olusegun Obasanjo who relinquished power as planned by his predecessor, Mohammed, to Alhaji Shehu Shagari, Gen. Ibrahim Badamosi Babangida and Gen. Sani Abacha schemed all Nigerians and while the former was in charge for eight years, the later wanted to change from khaki to mufti before his demise on June 8, 1998.

When Brig. Abacha announced the overthrow of the government of Alhaji Shehu Shagari, this was part of the declaration he made:

> "*The grave economic predicament and uncertainty which inept and corrupt leadership had impost ... can no more be tolerated.*"

The above is an example of coup announcement why a particular government should be changed and a call for transitional government made. But neither Gen. Ibrahim Babangida nor Gen. Sani Abacha and their cohorts could stand on their promise of handing over power to the civilians as soon as possible. The question is: did not these people rule this country with our so-called Christian brothers and sisters? Were they not partners in crime and looting to the army fellows? The examples they wanted to emulate -

and applied in this country, Nigeria include the following: Mobutu Sese Seko of Zaire, Gnassingbe Eyadema of Togo, Jerry Rawlings of Ghana, Col. Muammar Ghadafi of Libya, Samuel Doe of Liberia, to mention but a few. So Nigerians are lovers of power.

> ***It is unethical for a Christian to be so much power intoxicated that he may not want to relinquish his position for another person***

It is unethical for a Christian to be so much power intoxicated that he may not want to relinquish his position for another person. It is one of the worst things that have also contributed immensely in drawing Nigeria backward. Let us take the case of Lt.-Gen. Jeremiah Useni and Gen. Sani Abacha as examples, or Gen. Ishaya Bamaiyi. Gen. Jerry Useni parades himself as a Christian but without taking cognizance of the fact that he answers the name of one of the strongest pragmatic prophets of the old testament. He contributed immensely in persuading Gen. Sani Abacha to succeed himself. He also influenced the Traditional Rulers to take side and support Abacha.

The consequences or after-math of his activities was that instead of his being appointed the Head of State, at the expiration of Gen. Abacha as the most senior military man or army officer, he was by divine providence sidelined and dumped. His role in Abacha's self succession bid earned him no sympathy as he was forcefully thrown out of the military on the 28th of July 1998. The Bible says:

"*But seek first his kingdom and his righteousness, and all these things will be given to you as well,*"(Matt.6:3.)

Christians should not be worried about anything, but in prayers and supplications they should make their request known. We may also learn some lesson from the use of power wrongly that is recorded in I Kings 16:29 by Ahab and Jezebel his wife.

MONEY POLITICS

While all eyes are on politicians in countries like U.S.A. and Great Britain, watching where they got money for their campaigns and how much they spend, it is a reverse here in Nigeria. The reason is without spending huge sums of money, no one succeeds or wins an election. I have been within the corridor of political activities in Akwa Ibom State and Oron nation for about three years and I have drawn a conclusion that "money is politics and politics is money" in the Nigerian context.

For instance, for one to make an attempt of declaring his or her aspiration for an elected office from the Local Government level to the Presidency, he must have his money in stock, or somebody that is counting in millions must back him in providing the finances. To make a formal declaration an aspirant needs a lot of money to host the party stalwarts, other party members and the electorates. All is taken separately. He must 'settle' the Police Force, SSS, NECON now called INEC and other highly placed individuals including those in the then military administration, in order for one to have his way. M.K.O. Abiola and even Chief Matthew Olusegun Obasanjo would not make it without spending billions of Naira during their electioneering campaigns.

Another set of 'Christian' in the like of Chief Arthur Nzeribe, Mr. Daniel Kanu of the five million men March in March, 1998 and other parochial and myopic sycophants caused problems that shook the foundation of Nigeria because of their love for money in 1993 and 1998 respectively. The two mentioned, even though one is a senator now are 'Christians so called not in works or deeds but traitors of other Nigerians. The Bible says that Christians should "be free from the love of money". Arthur Nwankwo puts it this way: "The acute monetization of political process is survival of the richest – provision of rice, beans, garri, stockfish and salt with naira notes" during elections.

There is no reason on earth while Christians should ask for money and sell their conscience and power of freewill before they elect who would lead them. It is because of this demand for money from political or elected office holders that politicians are pushed to borrow money from wherever they could for their campaigns after which they must pay back when elected.

Most of the party stalwarts must complain that either the Chairman of a Council, Councilors or those in higher offices do not give them regards due as those who contributed so much to the success or victory of such people. But one thing they forgot is that there was nothing they did for nothing; from the beginning to the end they ate a lot of goats, collected a lot of money from the said chairman before they did anything. They took all that the elected man could offer them as an appreciation before time and when the time came, they are often thrown into the bush and looked down upon.

Christians should not be lovers of money and greedy, we are enjoined to choose from among the brethren one who should lead us.

"You shall surely set as
king over you, him whom

the Lord your God will choose. One from among your brethren you shall set as king over you; you may not set a foreigner, who is not your brother, over you. But he shall not multiply horses to himself or cause the people to return to Egypt in order to multiply horses, since the Lord said to you, you shall never return that way. He shall not multiply wives … silver and gold … he shall write for himself a copy of this law in a book, out of what is before the Levitical priests." (Deut. 17:15-20)

There is no reason on earth while Christians should ask for money and sell their conscience and power of freewill before they elect who would lead them.

Even though we know that money answers everything, the love of money is the root of evil,' and money can never be everything. That is why we often made mistakes of electing wrong people into public offices through money power only for them to enrich themselves without minding the predicaments of the poor masses. They also always paid for it because what we sow is what we reap.

MILITARY COUP/DICTATORSHIP

Military coup is another canker worm that destroys Nigerian politics and in the light of this I will quote some coups speeches which the military have not been able to properly execute when they succeed. Major Kaduna Nzeogwu on January 15, 1966, said "our enemies are political profiteers, swindlers, men that seek bribes, ... We seized power to stamp out tribalism, nepotism and regionalism". Major Gen. Aguiyi-Ironsi succeeded him since the young man did not get full control of the nation. The same government was toppled on July 29, 1966 in a counter coup.

When Lt. Col. Yakubu Gowon, as he was then, took over, he said that the country had been "plunged into a national disaster ... elimination of political leaders and that there is no base for political, economic as well as social unity." On July 29, 1975, another group struck led by Gen. Murtala Muhammed and he later became the Head of State, and on his address to the nation said, "that the government of Gowon lacked consultation, was indecisive, indiscipline and even negligent. The nation was being plunged inexorably into chaos." The man tried to stamp out corruption in Nigeria but was assassinated by another army officer Lt. Col. Buka Suka Dimka. It is on record that Gen. Mohammed was not a bad leader but was in full control of the military, political and administrative classes.

On February 14, 1976, Lt. Gen. Olusegun Obasanjo took over and though a reluctant leader, he set up a "government of transition" from the military to democratic order. He retired respectfully, he was neither killed or -

kicked out of office. "Mohammed and Obasanjo chose to leave politics for politicians and soldiers to soldierly things. Obasanjo left office for a democratically elected government of Alhaji Shehu Shagari on October 1, 1979. What he sowed in 1979 he also reaped in 1999, 20 years after.

> ***"Mohammed and Obasanjo chose to leave politics for politicians and soldiers to soldierly things***

The presidential government of Shagari was over thrown on December 30, 1983 since he wanted to stay on even when he did not perform well in his first tenure. Brig. Sani Abacha described the taking of that government as "bloodless and painstaking operations." The next day Major General Mohammadu Buhari was appointed the Head of State. Sani Abacha on his first broadcast of the coup said, "the grave economic predicament and uncertainty which an inept and corrupt leadership had imposed necessitated the taking over by the military," The government launched "War Against Indiscipline" (WAI), it was observed –

only in words but not in principle.

Major-Gen. Buhari was ousted from office on August 27, 1985 by Babangida when his point man Maj-Gen. Tunde Idiagbon was in Mecca on a pilgrimage. An address earlier by Brig. Joshua Dogonyaro stated that the government was overthrown that day. Major Gen. Sani Abacha later stated in another address to the nation that the "past leadership (Buhari/Idiagbon) lacked the capacity and the capability of leading this nation out of its economic and social predicament." Major-Gen. Ibrahim Babangida, who became the longest serving Head of State was named as the President and the Commander-in-Chief of the Armed Forces of the Federal Republic of Nigeria.

After staying in power for eight years and the country was thrown into chaos, confusion and tension politically by the annulment of June 12, 1993 Presidential election won by Chief M.K.O. Abiola, Gen. Babangida bowed out of office on August 27, 1993. He and his cohorts appointed Chief Ernest Shonekan as the head of Interim National Government while Prof. Okon

Uya was appointed as the Chairman of NEC to conduct a fresh election. Gen. Sani Abacha the strongest military officer planted by Gen. Ibrahim Babangida and Northern Hegemony took over the government from Shonekan in a palace coup and called his government "a child of necessity." Some Christians rallied around him and he appointed them key officers in the worst government that ever existed in Nigeria and none of them could resign his office because of the evil that was going on. He took over in November 17, 1993. At a meeting with traditional Rulers on June 6, 1994, in Abuja, Gen. Abacha declared, "a true democrat is someone who abides by the rules of civilized behaviours, the rules of discourse, dialogue and consensus." But he did otherwise and prolonged his stay in office looking for a way to transmute himself into a civilian Head of Government as President until the Lord on that fateful morning told him,

> *"But God said to him, 'you fool! This very night your life will be demanded from you. There you will get what you have*

prepared for yourself. This is how it will be with anyone who stores up things for himself but is not rich toward God."
Luke 12:20-21 NIV.

That was how the Almighty God demanded the life from Abacha and saved this country from a grave disaster on His appointed day – June 8, 1998. It should and must be a day of lesson to all Nigerians and Christians in particular, that the "LORD is-in-charge."

Therefore, the issues of coups in Nigeria are selfish and greed motivated plus the mean of further acquisition of wealth by the military men and the civilians sponsors. After all, a Peugeot 504 car that was sold between N7,000.00 and N10,000.00 during Shagari's administration is sold at over N2,000,000.00. Ordinary Nigerians and civil servants who are not involved in any shady deals cannot afford to buy a car irrespective of position or rank at this point in time. Christians have been liberated by the blood of Jesus Christ and they should reject and not support evil government even if it means to resign ones appointment. Coups do not help Nigeria to grow at all.

> **Ordinary Nigerians and civil servants who are not involved in any shady deals cannot afford to buy a car irrespective of position or rank at this point in time**

Consequently, the military leaders always turned into dictators within a short time in office by refusing to do whatever thing they promised when they took over power. Abacha said on August 17, 1994 that:

> *"I must stress the unflinching commitment of this administration to an early return to a civil democratic rule. We know that there are skeptics regarding the sincerity of our intentions. But in the past months, we have endeavoured to assure the public and in fact the world at large of our sincerity and credibility."*

But was Abacha ever sincere to himself and to Nigerians and the world at large? He refused to implement the above statement and turned into a dictator with an iron fist on all his opponents including his friend M.K.O. Abiola and his wife Kudirat whom his government killed in 1996. So, whenever any government lacked accountability and critics are not tolerated, such government is dictatorship. Such has been Nigerian government from 1960 till date.

Christians, learn your lessons for the dictatorship and the consequences from the lives of people like Pol Pot of Cambodia, Idi Amin of Uganda, Samuel Doe of Liberia, Mobutu of Zaire (now Democratic Republic of Congo) and even the iron fist of Gen. Sani Abacha who met his death while in bed. The Bible says, "Each of us will give account of himself." (Rom. 14:12 NIV.)

Fellow Christians the military coup and dictatorship are not the answer. We need democracy and to elect leaders with vision and development plan for our

Fellow Christians the military coup and dictatorship are not the answer

country. Remember, where there is no vision the people perish or die." Besides the above, a lot of prominent Nigerians have been killed through coups.

Coup is unchristian and unethical for Christian to be involved or be partakers of coups and to share in government of dictatorship. Absolom was one of David's most handsome sons, but when he thought he should take over power from the father and started campaigning at the gate, he was digging his grave – 2 Sam. 18. When Lucifer, the most beautiful angel also planned to take over some power from God, he also made a terrible mistake of his life. All authority is from God. Rom.13:1 and it is God who raises up and also brings down – 1 Sam.2:6. Therefore, the idea of people looking for power through coup is unethical even in the military and a dictator is an ungodly person. When the righteous is on the throne, the people rejoice but not so with the wicked. The Bible says, –

We are aware of hundreds of noble Nigerians both military and civilians who died as a result of coup and dictatorship.

"Righteousness exalts a nation, but sin is reproach to a people." Prov.14:34. We are aware of hundreds of noble Nigerians both military and civilians who died as a result of coup and dictatorship. Be warned and do not be a party to any coups.

TRADITIONAL RULERS

According to Chief Dr. Edet Amana in his book "*We can Take our People Up There.*" - Traditional Rulership has been the object of intense debate and according to him is why there are some wishes to see them as anachronistic and feudalistic. But others see value in the continued Traditional rulers in act of governance. Chief Amana further explained that "Traditional Ruler ship can be engineered to provide the much needed link between the tradition and culture of our people and the modern democratic system." In other words, traditional rulers are supposed to be links between the government and a particular group of people on matters that relate to the traditions and culture of the people and not to be partisan politicians. Their position should be that of a father whose many children may struggle for elected offices or positions.

It is a shameful thing that in recent times the traditional ruler ship has been turned into object of ridicule and instead of being appointed into that office by the people of a particular group or ethnic nationalities, their appointment comes from the government and they are given certificates of recognition by the same government. Gen. Ibrahim Babangida used his position while in government to appoint Alhaji Ibrahim Dasuki as the Sultan of Sokoto, but Gen. Sani Abacha dropped or deposed the Sultan of Sokoto, and enthroned Alhaji Mohammadu Maccido as his successor. What was Babangida's business with the Sultanate and what too was Abacha's business? As a result of this infringement, the paramount rulers are seen as mere puppets to the politicians as it is now. This is why they take side in matter in which they were supposed to be neutral as father of -

> ***the paramount rulers are seen as mere puppets to the politicians as it is now***

all. Accordingly, Arthur Nwankwo opines that, "many traditional rulers rather than becoming islands of neutrality and stability in the turbulent political climate... made themselves tools of political debauchery and victimization."

When Dasuki as the head of the Islamic faith in Nigeria first supported that Abiola should be given the people's mandate to rule, the whole nation applauded him, but the same Dasuki also turned round to say that it was not the will of Allah for Abiola, M. K. O. to be the president of the Federal Republic of Nigeria. Hence, he supported the annulment of June 12, 1993 presidential election, which was the freest and fairest election ever, conducted in this country. That annulment was an injustice. Shakespeare in his book Macbeth,' said "To be thus is nothing, but to be safely thus." Alhaji Dasuki thought all was well with him as a Sultan of Sokoto but shortly from that time he was deposed, dethroned and banished from the Sultanate by Gen. Sani Abacha. He was detained outside his domain.

Furthermore, the Chairman of Enugu

State Traditional Rulers' Council also played a terrible politics which did not work out well for him because the Almighty God was not happy with the role he was playing for Abacha's succession bid. He was the first Paramount Ruler Abacha urged to make a pronouncement that he (Gen. Abacha) should succeed himself and later joined by other traditional rulers from South Eastern State Geo-political Zone. All of them I believe were Christians. But God worked wonders and took away from Eze Nnaji the life in him that belonged to God. Consequently he died miserably in his hotel suite at Abuja while on business pursuit with Gen. Abacha even before the expiration of Gen. Sani Abacha. The Bible says, "Do not be deceived, God is not mocked, whatever we sow, we shall reap." Both Eze Nnaji and Abacha reaped what they sowed, Since they wanted to throw Nigeria into another civil war and bloodshed in Abacha's self succession bid, God took their lives. Is not God wonderful and terrible to be feared?

Nowadays, in Nigeria, some traditional rulers are also involved in the business of obtaining by tricks (OBT). They receive money from the politicians of all sorts and pledge to support them along side with their subjects but varnish into thin air immediately they get the money. Some do not see issue within their domain and Nigeria as a whole with a fatherly eye but with monetary interest. What a mess to some of these royal men who now behave like rustic and crude men. While their forebears sold fellow Nigerians out for slavery in exchange for a little sum of money to the colonial masters, they are now selling their subjects out, as did Esau for just one spoon of pottage, who sold his birth right to his younger brother. Some of them acted most of the time like illiterates who are simple to be induced with money and taken captive. Their forefathers sold their subjects out for slavery on just a little token from the white men. Nigerians are now slaves in the hands of their fellow countrymen because of the attitudes of some traditional rulers or leaders. Shame and big shame to some of the members of this institution who are collectors of bribes and executors of injustice. The wicked shall not go free.

IMPOSITION AND ELECTION RIGGING

Another factor that has adversely affected Nigerian politics is imposition of candidates on both the party and electorates plus election rigging. My practical example on that is based on that which took place in Urue Offong/Oruko Local Government Area, in Akwa Ibom State and my Local Government of Origin in which one Mr. Remigius Asukwo was imposed on the people from the party's level. This man was allegedly disqualified by NECON, SSS and POLICE during the screening exercise of candidates, as a man who failed to properly declare his assets among other things. But he was imposed on both the party – UNCP and on the entire people of Urue Offong/Oruko Local Government Area. A professed Christian he failed to perform as Chairman and is recorded as one of the worst in that office since the creation of the Local Government Area in 1991.

He was more than a dictator and military man in character. He ordered that I, the writer of this book, a Reverend gentleman whom he suspected did not support him to be the Chairman to be arrested and detained by -

the Police in the Police Force Headquarters in Uyo, Akwa Ibom State. This was when I was appointed by the students of my Local Government as a Caretaker Chairman of the National Association of Urue Offong/Oruko Students. He blackmailed me and other students appointed into the Committee as members of the secret cult and sent his petition to force Headquarters. I was given an opportunity to bail myself out the following day. What I am trying to say at this point is that the man did not pass through screening exercise, nomination and election in a proper way. His actions while in office justify the assessment of his official performance.

Besides the above, there is always a massive kind of rigging in Nigerian elections at all levels. An instance is that of April 25, 1998 National Assembly election. The turn out was very poor but all the ballot papers were thumb printed by just a few people after officials of NECON,POLICE and Party Agents

The turn out was very poor but all the ballot papers were thumb printed by just a few people after officials of NECON POLICE and Party Agents had received money from candidates and sold out their conscience

had received money from candidates and sold out their conscience. Like Arthur Nwankwo says, "Nigerian elections are always characterized by massive fraud, rigging, award of figures, falsification of results and untoward electoral practices." But God says in his word that *"I hate every false way"* (Ps.119:128 ASV).

A Christian should note that God does not associate Himself with anything that is false, crooked, manipulated or maneuvered. When the Apostles needed a replacement of somebody else in place of Judas Iscariot, all they did was to pick out two men who were qualified as eye witnesses of the deeds of Jesus Christ and after praying, they cast lots and Matthias was elected – Acts 1:24. The choice of deacons was not carelessly conducted but men of good repute, full of the Holy Spirit and of wisdom were appointed – Acts 6:1-6. They did not use foul methods, sentiments, greed, selfishness and the essence of looting of government's purse as it is done in Nigeria. Christians should avoid imposition and elections rigging at all cost because we shall give account of all our deeds.

HUMAN RIGHT ABUSES

Human Right abuses is another serious problem militating against a decent politics in Nigeria. The dignity of every human being is not respected in Nigeria in accordance with the provision of the nation's constitution and the United Nations Declaration of Human Rights of 10th December, 1948. Nigerians are not allowed to exhibit their freedom of expression and association without being arrested and detained by those in power. Nigerians are arrested at random by the so called Security Agents without being told the reason for such arrest or where they are being taken to.

Lawyers themselves are afraid of venturing into defending culprits or victims of government officials and those in authority

You do not need to ask them (Security) why you are under arrest and the warrant for your arrest and detention. Lawyers themselves are afraid of venturing into defending culprits or victims of government officials and those in authority. The Judiciary is (was) in a complete blunder. Judges, Magistrates and even private -

legal practitioners are being dictated to by the government in power.

Furthermore, where they do not want to arrest some, they go all out for their lives. There are recorded cases of assassinations and crack down on the opponents of those in power on daily basis. Few examples are; the set up or framed up plan against Lt. Gen. Oladipo Diya and others. Both Lt. Gen. Ishiaya Bamaiyi and Lt. Gen. Oladipo Diya who are still alive are Christians but their game in the military and Nigerian Politics was completely out of line with the love of Christ. There are the letter bomb sent to late Mr. Dele Giwa of Newswatch Magazine in 1986; the framing up Mrs. Chris Anyanwu, Bola Ige whose rights were taken away because of his utterances, and Chief Don Etiebet who was forced to dump his aspiration to become the President of the Federal Republic of Nigeria. Others who were forced into exile because they criticized the government. As Prof. N. S. S. Iwe quoted in his book – Socio-Ethical issues in Nigeria. "All

All human beings are born free and equal in dignity and rights

human beings are born free and equal in dignity and rights. They are endowed with reason and conscience and should act towards one another in a spirit of brotherhood." Human Rights abuses in Nigeria should be a matter of concern to the Christians. Remember we should do unto others what we wish should be done unto us.

However, even if those in authority do not respect our rights, we should always express to them what is right, good and honourable. After all the Bible says:

> "*For God did not give us a spirit of timidity (of cowardice, of craven and cringing and fawning fear), but (He has given us a spirit) of power and of love and of calm and well balanced mind and discipline and self control.*"
> (2 Timothy 1:7 Amplified Bible).

We should not be afraid of the mortals who can only destroy or kill the flesh and not the spirit or soul but we should fear him who is able to destroy both. Why then should Christians not be liberated from the evils of this country?

It is absolutely unchristian and unethical for Christians to run after their enemies in order to harm or intimidate them. As Christians we should encourage and exhibit respect for Human Rights. These are right to life, right for Human dignity, right of Association, right of expression,

> ***President Mobutu Sese Seko of Zaire and Pol Pot of Cambodia were megalomaniacs, both paid dearly for what they did to their fellow human beings, dying in shameful state and condition outside their domain***

right to education, Right to choice of vocation and human labour and right of the Media etc. People who are involved in the abuses never run away without paying for it – example. President Mobutu Sese Seko of Zaire and Pol Pot of Cambodia, both paid dearly for what they did to their fellow human beings, dying in shameful state and condition outside their domain. Remember that our God is no respecter of any person and none can escape his judgment. Be warned.

TRANSITION PROGRAMMES TO CIVILIAN RULE

The so called 'Transition Programmes' except that which was logically concluded in 1979 when Alhaji Shehu Shagari was presented as being democratically elected by the government of General Olusegun Obasanjo (Rtd) and that which Gen. Abdulsalam Abubakar, a respectable army general conducted at the end of 1998 and early 1999 and decided to quite by declaring Chief Matthew Olusegun Obasanjo as Nigerian elected President, other transitions were fake and always ended in fiasco. Billions of Naira which could have changed the fortune of Nigerians was thrown into the programmes by godless leaders both Muslims and their Christian collaborators. Nigerians are always deceived into these fake transitions and the effect is that of transition from bad to worse governance and economic downturn. Transitions of degeneration and more adequately 'life to death' because a lot of people have paid for it with their lives. These have been the experiences of Nigerians from the leadership of General Yakubu Gowon, Gen. -

Ibrahim Babangida and Gen. Sani Abacha, the master executor and killer.

> *Christians should liberate themselves from the hands of the Pharaohs in Nigeria and resist them to the fullest*

T The programmes are full of hidden agenda and one in which the resources of this country have been wastefully squandered and mismanaged by both those in government, elites who turned sycophants for their pockets and terrible business men in the likes of Arthur Nzeribe and the late Justice Bassey Ikpeme, who are the originators and agents that were used in the annulment of June 12, 1993 election – the freest and fairest. Is Nzeribe not a Christian till date? Like Arthur Nwankwo rightly said, "the military use political power for greedy accumulation and mismanagement of national resources.' Hence the military transition programmes are not aimed at the democratization of the society but at the enthronement of a corrupt and sympathetic civilian regime.

Christians should liberate themselves from the hands of the Pharaohs in Nigeria and resist them to the fullest. "Resist the devil and he will flee from you" (James 4:7 NIV). I think the best Christians and other God-fearing Nigerians should stand before these Pharaohs and say "let my people go.'

SUPPORT FOR ANY GOVERNMENT IN POWER

Nigeria is pulled backward politically because of the people's support for any government in power – " AGIP" – be it through a bloody coup or bloodless coup as the case may be. Nigerians do not know which government is legitimate and should be accepted or rejected but instead, it is the politicians, they traditional rulers and even civil servants Christians among the most of them that would throng around coup plotters who took over power.

AIDS - meaning "Acquired Integrity Deficiency Syndrome."

It is a syndrome in the Nigerian context and in the words of Prof. E. M. Uka is also AIDS - meaning "Acquired Integrity Deficiency Syndrome." Government and individuals without integrity are supported to be leaders and in-charge of the most populous black nation in the world. This is done with monetary motives of the people concerned. Some Paramount Rulers as fathers of different ethnic nationalities would go around singing praises of those in authority to the detriment of their people. In February 1998, the late Gen. Sani Abacha invited Paramount Rulers to Aso Rock Villa and after watching video clips of the framed coup plot allegedly led by Gen. Diya, they all joined their voices together in condemning Diya and others even before they were found guilty by the Kangaroo tribunal. The paramount rulers went away with car gift each from Gen. Abacha. The Sultan of Sokoto was given "Limousine Mercedes Benz E320. All other leaders of Traditional Rulers from State councils received a Mercedes Benz E 200 each." What a waste in our economy, while millions do not have one square meal in a day. Nigerians, according to Dare Babarinsa, "Have put their fatherland under the government of coup plotters by coup plotters and for coup plotters."

CHAPTER SIX

NIGERIANS AND DEVELOPMENT

"Let Go of whatever makes you STOP"
John L. Mason.

What truly can be diagnosed as the problems surrounding the development of African countries with particular reference to Nigeria, our country? Can we refute the fact that we are not among the nations blessed richly by God Almighty through human and mineral resources? You, I mean you the reader, are you not among those God has chosen to lead this country on the path of development? John Mason is of the opinion that you should; "Let Go of whatever makes you STOP" Let it go, greediness, selfishness, embezzlement, diversion of public funds for what it was meant for to individual purse, let go ethnicity, let go your parochial spirit, let go your euphoria and help Nigeria to be what she was meant to be by God. Let it truly be true that Nigeria is the giant of Africa – leading other African nations.

"In him we were all chosen, having
been predestined according to the

plan of him who works out everything in conformity with the purpose of his will." (Ephesians 1:11 NIV).

> *Do you not know that a very great number of Nigerian youth are doing menial jobs in countries we are greater than in all aspects?*

In God Nigeria and all of us in Nigeria have been predestined according to his plan and not ours – the plan through Christ Jesus to lead other African nations. But are we truly leaders? How and why? Do you not know that a very great number of Nigerian youth are doing menial jobs in countries we are greater than in all aspects? Do you know that hundreds of Nigerian youths if not thousands are working as slaves in neighbouring countries like Cameroon and even many of them perishing when confronted by wind storm on the high sea or Atlantic Ocean? Do you know?

What has happened to the billions of barrel of oil drilled and exported from Nigeria since oil was discovered in Nigeria? What have we done with the blessing of agricultural products? What about the industries, which you have personally helped to be grounded? What about our steel industries? If God is what he is and his purposes and plan unchangeable, I think you will let go of whatever makes you to stop'. I think it was some reasons similar to that of Nigeria but not on the context of development such as it is lacking in Nigeria at this time that makes St Paul to render this prayer not to the Ephesians again but to Nigerians:

> *"I keep asking that the God of our Lord Jesus Christ, the glorious father, may give you the spirit of wisdom and revelation, so that you may know him better. I pray also that the eyes of your heart may be enlightened in order that you may know the hope to which he has called you, the riches of his glorious inheritance in saints, and his comparably great power for us who believe. That power is like the working of his mighty strength, which he exerted in Christ when he raised him from the dead and seated him at his right hand in the heavenly realms, far above all the rule, and authority, power and*

dominion, and every title that can be given, not only in the present age but also in the one to come." (Ephesians 1:15-21, NIV).

We need to be enlightened in doing good, the eyes of hearts should be opened to see the plight of hardship other Nigerians are passing through

We need to be enlightened in doing good, the eyes of hearts should be opened to see the plight of hardship other Nigerians are passing through so that they may not only wait for the glorious hope in Christ but here and now, in the world that was created and is owned by their God. Brother think about underdevelopment of your village, Local Government Area, State and the nation as a whole. Think about your position and that of your people and remember "to whom much is given will much be required".

HOUSING

As you walk across some major streets especially in Lagos, you will discover that at points where fly-over roads or bridges are constructed, even under foot bridges, Nigerians without home and hope took their abode. Those who are in positions of buying and owning one or more houses are those in which houses are allocated or given. The 'oppressed creatures' as Karl Marx called them are those in which government does not have any plan for. No home, he is under the bridge, what right attitude can he develop under the bridge? Where is the promised housing for all in the Year 2000 by the Government?

I think it is high time for those in authority, I mean you my brother or sister, you Christians who were opportune to study abroad and exposed to the treatment given to citizens, even to you as a foreigner, to rise. Your plan should have been to help this country to do same. Let me tell you the truth, even though you may own housing estates and buildings, mansions as expensive as Aso Rock Villa, you can only sleep in one room at one corner at a time. You will only occupy just one small part of the big bed and not spreading yourself to cover the two family size foams or mattresses joined together to create a stadium bed for you.

I want to challenge people who are in the works and housing ministry to begin to develop plan to build housing estates even if it is a one room self contained for as many as can not afford to live in a bigger house. With the resources God has given this country this can be possible because with God all things are possible. Remember that Christ did not fail to say a word regarding our attitude to the homeless and those who are hungry:

> *"Then he will say to those on his left, 'Depart from me, you who are cursed, into the eternal fire, prepared for the devil and his angels. For I was hungry and you gave me nothing to eat, I was thirsty and you gave me nothing to drink, I was a stranger and you did not invite me in, I need clothes and you did not clothe me, I was sick and in prison and you did not look after me."* (Matthew 25:41-46 NIV.)

There is no post of responsibility my brothers and sisters without accountability. Do something today and change the condition of your fellow countrymen and women and you will receive the blessings of God.

AGRICULTURE

Nobody, absolutely nobody has been able to transform primary agricultural production of this country into agro-allied industries. Policy makers and executors are both the same – what to get out of it and not what the generality of people would have out of it is what matters. Even the fact of producing large quantities of palm kernel and oil, cocoa, rubber and groundnuts both for local consumption and export does not show the developed nature of agricultural sector. In the words of Arthur Nwankwo in his book: "Nigeria: The Political Transition and The Future of Democracy;"

> "*Exported cattle come back to the country as corn beef. Exported cocoa returns to our shores as chocolate drinks. Exported rubber comes back as wax, gum etc. The same for groundnuts, beniseed and cotton. It* is only when cocoa drinks are produced in commercial and exportable quantities in Nigeria, *milk making industries start flourishing and*

cosmetic factories that use raw palm products are fully developed that serious agro-allied industrial business will have begun in Nigeria.

> ***There has never been anything like continuity in any project embarked upon by an administration which the succeeding administration will see anything good in***

Imagine the number of people in Nigeria who by means of education have acquired knowledge on different forms of agricultural field without actually being used by the government and policy makers to develop that sector of our economy. Different names on agricultural projects embarked upon by the Federal Government have been coined over the years – Operation Feed the Nation, Back To Land, River Basin Authority etc, but are the projects today not being wasted and the equipments and buildings vandalized? There has never been anything like continuity in any project embarked upon by an administration which the succeeding administration will see anything good in. Public money that belongs to both the rich and the poor, the educated and uneducated, south and north becomes the property of just few opportunists.

There is nothing to ride home about in relationship with the agricultural sector of our economy. There are signboards of agricultural development project in all the States of the Federation but what actually comes out of that is not known. The Local Government cannot develop any agricultural ventures of their own to boost even local food production for consumption in their areas. The issue of fish farming, animal farming, production of palm oil and kernel is only left in the hands of peasants and few rich men who are interested in such things. Look at a small country like Malaysia and how the country's economy is thriving through their palm produce agro-allied industry. We have so turned our eyes to petroleum and crude oil that what would have contributed immensely into taking this country to her rightful position has been abandoned.

We have so turned our eyes to petroleum and crude oil that what would have contributed immensely into taking this country to her rightful position has been abandoned

Up till this moment about 80% of food production in this country is through crude farming methods. Policy makers have not created any avenue to help the farmers to flourish in their food production, which may have been developed into being exported as finished goods.

In Local Government levels, fertilizers sent to all the Local Council Areas in Nigeria are sold in transit to people who are not from the Local Council they were sent to. Shame and big shame that what each council would have used for Local Food production never-ever reached their destinations. The issue of Land Use Decree 1978 which would have been used in boosting food production only helped in giving the bourgeoisie the power to acquire choice areas of the cities for personal use. I am in support of Arthur Nwankwo in advocating that:

> *"A much more innovative and revolutionary approach has to be adopted with regard to the issues of farm settlement, the solving of the land tenure system, the mechanization of agriculture, large scale farming and land ownership. Unless these are done, the dream of the present generation of Nigerians for the development of agro*

based industries will remain a mirage."

Dear Executive Chairman of Local Council, Your Excellency, the Governor, Honourable member of State House of Assembly and National Assemblies. The President of the Federal Republic of Nigeria, I encouraged you in the words of John L. Mason that:

> *"You must be uncommon to be a champion. Your responsibility is not to remake yourself, but to make the absolute best of what God made. Don't compromise yourself... it's all you have got."*

STEEL PRODUCTION

It is clear that before there could be scientific and technological revolution, which lead to the creation of an industrial base, there must be steel production, especially by the production of flat sheets. It is a sine quo non for industrialization. We have scientists in this country and a lot of Nigerians have been exposed educationally into what could throw the country into being self reliant industrially but where are they and what has the government been spending our God given wealth in this direction?

Some years ago, the government of the Federation embarked on a steel project in Ajaokuta pushing billions of naira into it. This was a good venture and such that would have helped the country's industrial base to stand firm and rooted. Like every projects that are executed by the government from the Local Council to State and to the Federal Government, this precious project met its waterloo not long since it took off. Nigerians appointed into running this noble venture soon jumped into the 'chopping' side of the fence and soon the steel development project got paralyzed and then came the buying back of debt scam of the Abacha's administration being

Nigerians appointed into running this noble venture soon jumped into the 'chopping' side of the fence and soon the steel development project got paralyzed and then came the buying back of debt scam of the Abacha's administration being supervised by one Mr. Tony Ani and co

supervised by one Mr. Tony and co.

Brothers and sisters, without industrial development of our country in this 21st

Century, and by the time price of petroleum products may not give us much, we shall be wallowing in darkness and then we shall say, 'had I known'. This is the right time for us to know that we must build a better country for posterity. We know that the uses of steel are numerous. Almost all machine tools, engine parts, vehicle bodies, household utensils and cutlery, building materials etc. are made from steel.

> ***It is never too late for Nigeria to be what it should be. President Olusegun Obasanjo's administration if willing can put Nigeria into the path of development***

I think we do not know where we are going because which ever road we seem to have entered is full of inconsistencies. It is never too late for Nigeria to be what it should be. President Olusegun Obasanjo's administration if willing can put Nigeria into the path of development. ***Let his traveling all over the world not be just to open up a Super Market of imported items into Nigeria's market and economy but let it be that of pushing the***

country into industrial development. I solicit that the Federal Government should set up a standard research center for Nigerian researchers and let it be that researchers in all the fields should be encouraged to take up the challenges before them. More so, let those who can by one way or the other invent anything be encouraged by their being supported financially for a better development of what they have invented. I am convinced duly that inventions were not just God's personal or colour gift to the white people and Western world.

According to Lord Chesterfield as quoted by John Mason:

> *Firmness of purpose is one of the most Necessary sinews of character and one of the best instruments of success. Without it, genius wastes his efforts in a maze of Inconsistencies.*

Let Nigeria no longer be like a man without direction. Let us help ourselves while it is yet day for the

> *Let us help ourselves while it is yet day for the night comes where no one can see in order to act*

night comes where no one can see in order to act. The human resources in this country are enormous but are they being used or utilized effectively?

If you do not have a vision for your life, then you probably have not focused in anything. (Dr. David Burns). Let us have a big vision for our country and take her to her God given position in Africa and in the world. Nobody can in ernest do this except you and I.

PETRO-CHEMICAL INDUSTRIES

Fellow Christians even though I write some of these items as a lay man, I want us to also consider the idea of helping our country to truly develop her petro-chemical industries. By this I do not mean the industries in which goods already produced would be imported only to be re-labelled. Petro-chemical products are very vital in economic self-reliance and development of industrial base, if petroleum and chemical are used as components, raw materials for pharmaceutical, textile, plastic-making and other industrial items could be produced.

> ***For you to have been chosen is no mistake except you make it so and nobody may have been suitable at this point in time than yourself***

Car manufactu-ring plants chemical industries and even breweries could be possible through petro-chemicals. Let us consider this aspect of development and embark in developing petro-chemical industries. We need it. Engineers,- mechanical, chemical, electrical, electronics and every other form of engineering work should make their contributions. But I want to say that policy makers that are **not** politicians who are in authority are in better positions to bring this to pass. For you to have been chosen is no mistake except you make it so and nobody may have been suitable at this point in time than yourself. You know that the wages of sin is death: If you allow the joy of the Lord to be your strength God will definitely help you to fulfill your God-given destiny. Let us think of what we have to do for this country and not what we can get out of it. There are not limit to our possibilities.

Doing something that will save others should be a thing of great joy to Christians because no one really expect more than he has given out. Mother Theresa as quoted by John Mason once said, 'unless life is lived for others it is not worthwhile'. A self-centred life is totally empty.

A kind man benefits himself
But a cruel man brings trouble
On himself – (Prov. 11: 17 NIV)

Your own soul is nourished
When you are kind; it is
Destroyed when you are cruel.
(Prov. 11: 17 TLB.)

Think about what questions you will be asked at the close of your life on earth. Nathan Schaeffer as quoted by John Mason in his book "*Let Go of whatever makes you stop.*" Says

The question will not be, How much have
You got? But How much have you given?
Not How much have you won? But
How much have you done? Not How much
Have you saved? But How much have you
Sacrificed? It will be, How much have
you loved and Saved? Not, How much
were you honoured?

> ***Measure your life with what you have given and not by how long you lived or its duration***

So what ever you got, whatever you won, whatever you saved and whatever honour or honours you have received from men especially sycophants and praise singers who are only helping you to perish, some blank spaces of not giving, not doing, not sacrificing and not serving will be written all over you and that you know leads to condemnation. Measure your life with what you have given and not by how long you lived or its duration. Have a good attitude about your fellow countrymen and women and have that attitude too towards mankind. The world is not yours but it can be if you can leave your footprint on the sands of time in your locality. I am not saying the world will be called your world but you will be remembered in all generations. Note that people like Herbert Macaulay, Nnamdi Azikiwe, Obafemi Awolowo and Anthony Enahoro can never be out of the history of this country for good as long as the world is in existence. Let us renew our minds toward doing what is good for our country.

Remember the world is not yours and for the fact that you acquired much wealth today does not mean that your children will be wealthy people in future. It is rather better to acquire wealth that will last for ever and that is eternal life. Brethren, the Bible says:

> *Let us not become weary*
> *in doing good for at the*
> *proper time we will reap*
> *a harvest if we do not give*
> *up. Therefore as we have*
> *opportunity, let us do good*
> *to all people especially to*
> *those who belong to the families of believers.*
> (Galatians 6: 9,10.)

> ***for the fact that you acquired much wealth today does not mean that your children will be wealthy people in future***

Surrender your mind to Jesus Christ, asking for direction as you direct others in planning for the good and well being of others. If your position is associated with both authority and power use both to do good to others and you shall receive your reward or harvest in due time. People who are encouraging you to loot because they say it is your time or turn are not helping you in any way, they are the same people who will expose your activities and how you looted to the world. Do you hear me? It is your friends who would expose you to the pressmen and they are those who will condemn you. Think about that and think wise. It is rather good to listen to God than men for at the end they will make caricature of your personality.

ELECTRICITY/POWER

It is a very sad issue that the giant of Africa and the most populous black nation in the world cannot generate a constant power supply at all times. The nation has continued to groan in darkness without solution for power supply from Never Expect Power Always (NEPA). Is Nigeria and Nigerians passing through this horrible thing because they cannot afford electrical engineers that can manage the authority effectively? The answer is NO. Have Nigerians not live in Western world before where there has been nothing like power outage?

I think it is a shameful thing even to some Christians who are among the saboteurs who are not ready to allow anything to work out for the good of others. The country can even at this point generate power and supply it to other neighbouring countries but allocation and supply of power is difficult to handle in Nigeria. Towns and cities in which more power is in demand are the cities in which proper allocation is denied and those cities in which nothing absolutely is done with electricity are the cities in which supply of power is adequately allocated and supply. But note that those who walk in darkness can never see the light. Some because of their economic well-being do not give a damn to whatever is happening within this sector of Nigerian life because they can afford generating plants all over their buildings – in the villages, cities and offices.

> ***Do not be party to whatever has been keeping this country in darkness and backward-ness***

Christians, be faithful ambassadors of Christ and represent Him well wherever you find yourself. Do not be party to whatever has been keeping this country in darkness and backwardness. This country is ours and whatever we make of it today shall stand for or against us in posterity. Keep the country moving on the right path and shun all that tends to divide us as a people and nation. Shun ethnicity and parochialism, do unto others what you wish others do unto you. I want to point out to you that as somebody from Oron in Akwa Ibom State, an Igbo man paid for the first car I got and drove in life on my behalf and the man is from Abam in Arochukwu Local Government Area of Abia State. Methodist ministers may not have given me such help as that in which a Presbyterian minister Rev. Uche Kalu Ibe did. Why then must we continue to allow ourselves to be tied down by what in philosophy and logic is known as "Idol of the Tribe." We can explore more and more and get more if we work together as a team. Christian policy maker-members in NEPA look for a solution to your perpetually putting the country and people in darkness. We

> ***We can explore more and more and get more if we work together as a team***

cannot continue like this. There should be a change.

SOCIAL SECURITY

It is a very pathetic issue and problem that there is nothing like a social security and insurance for Nigerians. The so-called insurance are merely by name and the government does not in any way care for the down trodden and disabled people in our midst. People are not insured , they live their hopeless lives in the midst of those who are having the best of life. No money, no home, no food, no clothing and no future for them. The government is not in any way considerate of their plights – insanes, blinds, deafs and dumbs, cripples and other disabilities. Is there nothing government can centrally do for this group of people? Politicians and decision-makers, are there no ways this group could be helped? Think about it, if you were in their position and condition, what you would have felt like?

We have left so many things undone that I think God himself will judge us. All the resources from the petroleum products or –

crude oil which you and your cohorts have been enjoying

Why can you not use your position to effect a change in the lives of others

to the detriment of other Nigerians is not your personal property. It was not out of your doing or power that you are what you are today. It is just the GRACE OF GOD, it is not by power lest you should boast. Why can you not use your position to effect a change in the lives of others? Why can you not allow God to use you as His instrument of blessing in your generation so that you may be remembered throughout posterity?

God has not changed his plan concerning the second coming of His son and judgment. After all, 'it is appointed unto men once, to die and after that judgment..' Do you hear that the best solicitors or lawyers in the world will also stand trial and judgment? Remember that God is no respecter of any man. Think about what you should come out with for the people of Nigeria. Think about the conditions of some Nigerians and compare it to your own. Think -

about all that you have acquired through looting and conspiracy. Think about your role in whatever position you find yourself. Think about how corrupt you may have been and how many you have robbed of their God-given resources and good life. Remember that Jesus came that we may have life and even have it abundantly. Think about all that. If you have a very special touch in your spirit about our country and people simply say the word of this song:

1. Dear Lord and Father of mankind
   Forgive our foolish ways
   Reclothe us in our rightful minds
   In purer lives Thy service find.
   In deeper, reverence praise.

2. In simple trust like theirs who heard,
   Beside the Syrian sea:
   The gracious calling of the Lord
   Let us like them, without a word
   Rise up and follow thee.

3. Drop Thy still dew of quietness,
Till all our striving cease;
Take from our souls the strain and stress
And let our ordered lives confess;
The beauty of Thy peace.

4. Breathe through the heats of our desire,
Thy coolness and Thy balon;
Let sense be dumb, let flesh retire,
Speak through the earthquake wind and fire.
O still small voise of calm. Amen.

John Greenleaf Whithier
1807-92.

CHAPTER SEVEN

PRESENT AND FUTURE GENERATIONS

Do not think that I have come to abolish
The Law or the Prophets, I have not come
To abolish them but to fulfill them.
(Matthew 5:17 NIV)

It is true that Christians and denominations in its entirety do not accept and practice the same thing as recorded in the Bible – the Holy Book. While some will simply depend and adopt those things that are in the New Testament, others simply take what are in the Old Testament, while other denominations may accept both. The main problem is not just taking a part or a whole but that of watering done the pure gospel of Christ. Prosperity ministries has taken over the gospel of Holiness that people's ears itches when they are told to repent of their sins.

Jesus Christ in the above scripture says that he did not come to cancel the law or wipe it out but to confirm or fulfill it. And that whatever the Prophets said stands. For instance the 'soul that sinneth, it shall die." That is to say in the word of Jesus Christ, "repent or you will perish" or in the words of St. Paul, "the wages of sin is death." Jesus Christ was so blunt on the issue that he said in the next verse that all that is in heaven and earth will pass away but not an iota of God's word shall lack fulfilment.

> *For truly I say to you, until heaven and earth pass away, not the smallest letter or stroke shall pass away from the law until all is accomplished.*
>
> Matthew 5:18 NAS

I want to use this opportunity and medium to call on the present generation of Nigerians and indeed the future generation to shun the evil of our fathers and begin to face the challenges of the changing world with a visionary eyes. United States of America, France, Great Britain, Japan and even China to mention but a few in recent times would never have been what they are today without vision, follow-up and continuity of their forebear or ancestors. We have depended so much on the white man and his products, which we have refused to develop and make progress in any area except to depend on the colonial masters.

Just look at Japan before the 1945 bombing of Hiroshima during the Second World War and compare the Japan that we have today to the former one, the difference is clear, great development in all areas – significantly in automobiles – lovely cars and jeeps and in electronics, they are giants.

What on earth is the matter with African nations? Should we perpetually continue to live in darkness and poverty? Can you sit down and guess what our problems are? Do you not know that it is the leaders that are suppose to move the nations forward? Do you not know that a good driver drives the car in a good way and very well, whereas the bad and ignorant driver causes accident that may lead to the death of so many people? Do you not know that if somebody rises up today and challenge us by intimating the people on the path to self reliance, that something great will happen in this country within one decade?

Look let me tell you, our problem in the African nations or Nigeria is not calling on the Western nations to relief us of the debt owed them but "is" that of our saying to ourselves

"What do we do and where do we begin?" Where are the people who developed local bombs during the Nigerian-Biafra war? Where are the great brains of Nigeria? We destroyed the steel plant of Ajaokuta because myopic, parochial and uneducated leaders have been in charge. A blind man never leads a blind. Both will fall into a pit.

Christians, what do we do? Is there any way we can leave a legacy for our children and grand children? The natural resources are available, the human resources is adequate in the context of this discussion, the land mass is enough to build whatever we want to build but the problem is getting the Nehemiah who would decide to leave the King's rich palace to build the ruins of his fatherland.

NEHEMIAH WANTED!

Christians, man and men of actions are wanted right now in Nigeria. Pragmatic and charismatic leaders are wanted! Men with great visionary eyes are wanted! Lovers of their fellow men and fatherland are wanted. We should call it a day and night with the system of government called 'kleptocracy'. If politics as I better understand it is the gaining of power to pursue ideals, I am pleading with 'Christians' true and real 'Christians' with visions to rise and salvage our great country. Let us not be beggars again in the land of great abundance. We need Nehemiah at all cost.

Wait a minute. Who was Nehemiah? You will get to understand who Nehemiah was by picking your copy of Bible to read the book Nehemiah'. But let me give you a brief about him. Nehemiah must have been a Jewish son born in exile because about 100 years had elapsed before his action for his fatherland – Jerusalem. He grew up in a foreign land but had concern for his fatherland not minding what it might cost him to leave the pleasure of the King's palace to an unknown land which he originated from. While in the foreign land – Persia, his mind was at home, a small troublesome place far from the centre of power. He was what we may call today Personal Assistant (PA) of the King of Persia.

When Nehemiah heard of the problems or difficulties his people were experiencing, he took his career and his life – in his hands and spoke to the King about it. Then he started touring the broken down walls of the city by night, a city he probably had never seen before. About 100 years had gone by since his people returned to Jerusalem from exile, the temple had been rebuilt, but the city was partially occupied as most people decided to live in nearby cities and villages. The result was that the Israelites, the set apart people of God were so much mixed up with all kinds of foreigners. They were in danger of losing their identity. Why? Because the city lacked a wall, there was no security, they were married to all kinds of people, they were losing their own language, culture and most importantly, their religion. A wall was needed to give them a chance to make Jerusalem a truly Jewish city. We need a wall in Nigeria.

Firstly, against corruption. Thank God for the anti-corruption bill that was signed into law and which has started gaining momentum especially in the Upper National House of Legislature. Can, Chief Matthew Olusegun Obasanjo stand out to be the man that will lay foundation for the building of this wall? Secondly, such a leader must be pragmatic and used the best brains in this country to develop this country for posterity. We are tired of expatriates handling lots of projects in this country but I am sure that we also know that Nigerians because of the quest for money and wealth left so many projects uncompleted.

Let us go back and consider those qualities that were in Nehemiah. His personal memoirs shows that he was a great leader. He was an organizer, a pragmatic leader.

Nigeria like Jerusalem of Nehemiah's time could not progress because of local resistance to progress though some politicians used to call themselves 'progressives'. Powerful politicians in this country are always in the habit of frustrating government and calling on the military to take over power. I thank God that in the past 40 years of Nigeria's independence, we have all felt the iron hand of the military men and shall never again venture to call on them to take over power for our selfish ends.

Again Nehemiah showed remarkable qualities of a good leadership; impassioned speeches, prayer, organization, resolves, trust in

God, quick and determined response to problems, and unselfishness. Some people opposed and ridiculed his laudable venture at all course but he was determined in his heart to build the wall. When the opposition was gaining momentum, he called his nobles and officials and the rest of the people and said:

> "*Don't be afraid of them. Remember the Lord, who is great and awesome, and fight for your brothers, your sons and your daughters, your wives and your homes.*" (Nehemiah 4:14 NIV.)

He alerted the people of the development by opposers that was going on and did not call on them to fight for themselves but for their brothers, sons, daughters, wives and homes. The implication of that was that he encouraged them to fight for all. When your home alone is enjoying the pleasures of this country, what happens to your fellow country-men and brother? What about your sons, daughters and wives in future? Were Abacha to know the travail his family is going through since his demise globally and in Nigeria, I think his advise would have been that people and leaders should exhibit a good governance and life-style.

Nehemiah was a man of God. He was more than a manager. He did not act without prayer and he did not pray without acting. He recognized God's role in all that happened and never forgot to give God the credit. He was not looking for earthly status like the ones organized by most traditional rulers for political office holders in honouring them with one chieftaincy title or the other in order for them to extort some money from those guys. All that, tantamount to sycophancy in high places. Nehemiah would not have gone back to Jerusalem if he wanted status, good life and wealth.

Are you a Christian? Are you truly a Christian? Then if your answer is in affirmative, please rise and do something. Without a vision, the people perish and die but where there is vision there is life in abundance if not now but for posterity. Some people must have to do the sacrifice. Some people should show the way, people should be concerned. Where is the housing for all in the year 2000? Where is the free medical services for all in the year 2000? Where is the free education for all in the year 2000? Where is the goodness of life promised to all by evil governments in the year 2000? The year would soon be gone and yet things remain the same. God needs men and women like you and me. The harvest is great but the labourers are few.

Let me tell, you this plain truth. Your having 20 flashy cars today and a lot of estates across the world is never an assurance that your children and grand children will continue to live in abundance of life. After-all even an empire, like Roman empire, today is no more leading the world rather it is a place nobody ever thought of like U.S.A that is on the lead. I know a family or many families that were in abundance when the owner of the wealth was alive that are today living in penury even by selling out all the flashy cars and not even being able to afford a motorcycle. What am I saying? It is rather good to live a moderate lifestyle than acquiring wealth in which there will be no lasting happiness and abundance for a long time. Your being rich and wealthy does not make your children rich and wealthy. After all most dull brains in schools are students from very rich and extravagant families. Most of the children are trained in the best and most expensive Nursery schools and probably in the

Federal Government Colleges but these are the students that are mostly in secret cults, who cannot pass their examinations and 99% are into examination mal-practices. They pay for their marks and grades to greedy lecturers and can never defend their certificates.

We should begin to plan the type of Nigeria we want our children and children, children to live in. This is the time. Be involved in politics and make positive contributions. Shun greediness and selfish exhibition of power and authority. Your getting a Jet plane does not guarantee that your children will also have Jets. Think about the type of country you want them to live in. Plan the type of country you want for yourself and your people today. Somebody must begin and let the person be you. Your going with siren and convoy of about 20 cars today does not guarantee your going on that all the days of your life. Remember, it is a true fact that no condition is permanent.

> "Man born of woman is of few days
> and full of trouble."(Job 14:1 NIV.)

Your few days on earth is determined by God and there is no way with all your power that you can run away from trouble.

Brothers and sisters, we are the light of the world, a city built on a hill. We should allow people to see our good work and glorify God. We are the salt of the earth and should not allow our salt to lose its saltness. If we lose our saltness we shall definitely be good for nothing.

> "*Do not store up for yourselves treasures on earth where moth and rust destroy, and where thieves break in and steal. But store up for yourselves treasures in heaven, where moth and rust do noi destroy, and where thieves do not break in and steal. For where your treasure is, there your heart will be also*. (Matthew 6:19-21).

We store away billions of naira that belongs to the generality of the people, the money gotten from the wealth that God stored inside the earth for all in whom he gave the land. The Ogonis , the Ijaws, Akwa Ibomites and the rest of the oil lands are denied even good compensation to what belongs to them because of the obnoxious degree of land act that was promulgated some years ago.

Listen to this word of Jesus Christ:
"So in everything, do to others what you would have them do to you. For this sums up the Law and the Prophets." (Matthew 7:12).

Oga, councilor, chairman, member House of Assembly, Governor, member House of Representatives and Senate, President including all the commissioners and ministers with other political office holders, remember to do to others what you would have them do to you. You will definitely not be there forever. Plan good and do good and the good God shall bless you in all ways.

We should always remind ourselves that when the Bible says, that believers should not associate with unbelievers it does not say it in the sense of calling us out of the world in which unbelievers are also in existence. There is no way in which one can never have anything to do with unbelievers for we cannot avoid interacting with them on daily basis. In our homes, in our offices, when traveling they may be our driver or pilot, in the market we buy from them etc. In the translations of that scripture as recorded in Today's English Version.

> "Do not try to work together as equals with unbelievers, for it cannot be done. How can light and darkness live together? How can Christ and the devil agree? What does a believer have in common with an unbeliever? How can God's temple come to terms with pagan idols?" 2 Corinthians 6:14-16c.

The above is not forbidding us to work with them in our different fields of endeavours rather, we should not compromise with them on issues against our faith and believe in Christ. I think in the Nigerian context, we have been practicing the opposite of what the Bible says. Light and darkness can never be together at the same time and wrong and right cannot be partners or co-exist. Why we can do these things may not be through our power but of the extra-ordinary power of God in us as God's Holy Temple.

For we are the Temple of the Living God! And as regards the above, God Himself in his will said:

> "I will live with them and walk among

them, and I will be their God, and they will be my people. Therefore come out from among them and be separate, says the Lord. Touch no unclean thing and I will receive you. I will be a father to you and you will be my sons and daughter, says the Lord Almighty."

If we present ourselves as the temple, if we walk in accordance with his command by loving the Lord our God with all our hearts, minds and souls, and if we 'Love' our neighbours as ourselves, the will of God is that He will live and walk in our midst. He will be our God and we shall definitely be His people. The implications of God living, walking and sharing with us mean the blessing of God in its entirety. God is ever ready to be our God if we allowed Him and He is ready to lead us on the path of righteousness if we agree to do so.

When are we going to create a good and conducive environment for all to live in? When are we going to say no to corruption in order to help the downtrodden in our society? When can we make a "U" turn in order to move the country forward? When will you personally say to God use me as your instrument of blessing to mankind? When? Martin Luther King Jnr. Once said:

> "The quality not the length of one's life is what is important."

How old we may live and how much we have acquired is not what matters as we live in this planet earth but the quality and contributions we have made to our fellow men and women is important. Come out from among them and be separate and take a decision today about the type of society you envisage for your people in Nigeria as a nation. Give your life to Jesus and begin to see the plight of your fellow men with the eye of Jesus and you will have the compassion of Jesus in your heart.

> When he saw the crowds he had compassion on them, because they were harassed and helpless, like sheep without a shepherd. Then he said to his disciples 'The harvest is plentiful but the workers are few. Ask the Lord of the harvest therefore to send out workers into his harvest field". (Matthew 9:36-38 NIV.)

> Filled with compassion, Jesus reached out his hand and touched the man. 'I am willing, he said, Be clean! Immediately the leprosy left him and he was cured." (Mark 1:41 NIV.)

We should be compassionate in order to see what is good and right to be done for our fellow men. Jesus Christ was always full of compassion for people and that is what he is doing till to day. It is out of his compassion for us that her died on our behalf on the Cross of Calvary.

I know that we have been fasting and praying, calling on God daily for his blessing, declaring a solemn assembly even on the National level so that we can pray for our country being directed by a former Head of State – Gen. Yakubu Gowon. Nevertheless God has his own kind of fasting which is acceptable to him not just the assembly.

> "Is not this the kind of fasting I have chosen; to loose the chains of injustice and untie the cords of the yoke? To set the oppressed free and break every yoke. Is it not to share your food with the hungry, and to

provide the poor wanderer with shelter, when you see the naked, to clothe him and not to turn away from your own flesh and blood? Then your light will break forth like the dawn, and your healing will quickly appear; then your righteousness will go before you, and the glory of the Lord will be your rear guard. Then you will call, and the Lord will answer; you will cry for help, and he will say: Here am I. If you do away with yoke of an oppression, with the pointing of finger and malicious talk. And you spend yourselves in unbehalf of the hungry and satisfy the needs of the oppressed, Then your light will rise in the darkness, and your night will become like the noon day. The Lord will guide you always, he will satisfy your needs in a sun scorched land and will strengthen your frame. You will be like a well watered garden, like a spring whose waters never fail." (Isaiah 58:6-11).

I exhort you to read the above passage again and meditate upon every line of the passage and you will discover the secrets of God's blessing not mostly in our humility of fasting and praying in our closets or church it is that of breaking the Yoke of oppression and injustice. It is the giving of food and clothing for those in need. It is the provision of shelters for those without shelter. God has promised that if you do the above, your light will rise in darkness and your night like a noonday. That he will guide you and satisfy your need in a sun scorched land like Nigeria. You will be like a well-watered garden. What a wonderful promise of blessing to serve those in need.

If you are a politician you may not do these with your money but with the money that belongs to the people. We can also see that God is interested so much in making the condition of those who are hopeless into something full of hope. Any one who is into doing the services listed in Isaiah 58 to his fellow men shall be like a 'well watered garden'. But if you are into the business of looting, forget it, your portion will be the opposite – there shall be no light for you in darkness, your night will be tick darkness, the Lord will not guide you at all, the Lord will not satisfy your needs, the glory of God shall not be around you, you will be like a desert where there is no water, you will call and the Lord will not answer. Your money, your family, your friends, your health, your brothers and sisters and even so called 'loved one' will fail you. The consequence will be your latter position will be worst than the former. Listen, your latter position and condition will be worst.

CHAPTER EIGHT

"When you enter the land the Lord your God is giving you and have taken possession of it and settled in it, and you say 'let us set a king over us like all the nations around us,' be sure to appoint over you the king the Lord your God chooses. He must be from among your own brothers. Do not place a foreigner over you, one who is not a brother of Israelite. The King more over must not acquire great number of horses for himself or make the people return to Egypt to get more of them, for the Lord has told you, 'you are not to go back that way again. He must not take many wives, or his heart will be led astray. He must not accumulate large amounts of silver and gold."

When he takes the throne of his kingdom, he is to write for himself on a scroll a copy of this law, taken from that of the priests, who are Levites. It is to be with him, and he is to read it all the days of his life so that he may learn to revere the Lord his God and follow carefully all the words of this law and these decree and not consider himself better than his brothers and turn from the law to the right or to the left. Then he and his descendants will reign a long time over his kingdom Israel" (Deut 17:14-20 NIV.)

I would have concluded this book by the above scriptural quotation but I will be unfair to both myself and the readers of this book. We know that in the history of Israel, the appointment of leaders was solely done by God. At that time too, God was the one directing every affair of the Israelites from Moses to Joshua and succession of judges were chosen directly by the Lord to govern Israel on his behalf. Moses here, however, anticipates a time when the people would ask for a king contrary to the Lord's ideal for them. So Moses gives guidance concerning the eventual selection of a king. And the later king of Israel beginning from Solomon became guilty of what the Lord had instructed Moses about the king, except that they did not make Israel return to Egypt.

I have been opportune to discuss some political issues with Christians and discovered that in the first instance Christians do not trust or believe in themselves or fellow Christians as having the where-withal of ruling this nation. This is mainly so because for them somebody should bring money in the bag called '*Ghana must go*' for them to share before they could support the fellow. Mostly on Presidential elections.

The instruction is that when we want to choose a leader, the person must be our brother and not a foreigner. He must not be a squander maniac – acquiring great number of horses (flashy cars) and make the people to return to Egypt (sin). He must not run after many women or wives, which is what led to the death of our former dictator (Gen. Abacha), this also led him astray. He must not loot the nation's treasury-accumulating silver and gold (Naira, Pound Sterling and Dollars) for himself. He must put the law of God, the Holy Bible before him and he is to read it all the days of his life so that he may learn to revere the Lord his God and follow his word carefully. He must not consider himself as being superior or better than his brothers, which is one of the main _ practices in the Nigerian politics. Supporters of a winning politician in Nigeria are always dumped and forsaken by their friend when elected leader. I have seen this and it has caused a lot of problems in Nigeria, which may have resulted in the death of some people because "the soul that sinneth it shall die".

I was always wondering who the man Sergeant Barnabas Jabila is until the story about his background in Tell Magazine, No.14 April 3, 2000 was on the news stand. I was shocked to discover that Barnabas answered after the Barnabas in the Holy Bible and was from a Christian family of the North. This man with operational nickname of Sergeant Roger obeyed orders to the letter. He was close to power and was among those fearless boys who swore to protect Gen. Sani Abacha. Barnabas instead of becoming the prince of light became the prince of darkness who obeyed men rather than God. It was Barnabas who fired the bullets that killed Kudirat Abiola and some other noble Nigerians. He was a member of the Aso Rock fraternity of darkness without remembering his Biblical name – Barnabas. The truth of the —

matter is that the young man is indeed reaping his fruit of labour. This is because the God of justice who is no respecter of any man is paying them according to their deeds.

It is my earnest conviction that Christians are the majority in the socio-economic and political formations of Nigeria. They first had the Western Education before their Moslem brothers. But is seems we often forget what should be our standard kind of behaviour with regards to the paramount teachings of Christ as summarized below:

> "*You shall love the Lord your God with all your heart, and all your soul and with all your mind. This is the great and first commandment. And the second is like it, you should love your neighbour as yourself. On these two commandments depend all the law and the prophets.*" (Matt.22:37-40 ASV).

That was the main focus of Christ Jesus when he delivered his great sermon on the mount. "LOVE' unlimited, firstly directed to God which consequently reflects on our relationship with our neighbours. Barnabas did not put himself in the places of those he killed for Abacha to have known how painful that could have been for their family. This two fold commandments of Jesus Christ represents the summary of the ten commandments of God in the Old Testament – Exo.20:1-17. Prof. N. S. S. Iwe also has this as his comments:

> *Here is the two in one Christian commandment of love. Here is the supreme ethical pole of Christianity which vertically and teleological links human beings to their Creator as it forges bond of solidarity among them. Love is the core, the measure and judge of Christian life and morality.*

Do we earnestly love God and our neighbours? Without love, there can be no change in human motive towards every action taken. It is very real that anything that is not done out of love is contrary to the will of God and the ethics of Christ and Paul. A full breakdown of the type of love Christians should exhibit is recorded in I Cor. 13:1-13. It is evidenced in self sacrifice and sincere service of the neighbour and if this is transferred into action within the political arena imagine the type of society that will be in existence.

Consequently, upon the factors militating against putting in place an enduring democracy in Nigeria which I have treated in this book, Christians must note that without 'LOVE' these evils cannot be eradicated in Nigeria. Christians should live up to what their customs and habits should be. We are all aware of the fact that there is a complete breakdown of law and order in Nigerian society. Firstly by those in authority and secondly by the masses and the aftermath is indiscipline and irresponsibility both in high and low places.

Ethnicity, religious intolerance and riots like those associated with the *sharia* trouble that rocked this country, even to her foundation, on Monday 20th February, 2000 in Kaduna; corruption, love of wealth, love of power, money politics, military coups, dictatorship, election rigging and killing, Human Rights abuses, hidden agenda syndrome in transition programmes to civilian rule, support for any government in power, traditional rulers misrepresenting their subjects, and other political vices, should be matters of great challenge to the Christians. Christians should rise and fight or resist the vices in a most offensive way. Resist the devil and he will flee from you. Gen. Olusegun Obasanjo, after his release from prison custody, and before becoming the President of the Federal Republic of Nigeria on May 29, 1999, told Nigerians this:

> "*But there is no reason to fear the wicked and the ungodly because if they kill the body, they cannot kill the soul. Evil will not thrive if good people rise up collectively against it. What evil persons fear most is exposure and what they desire most is praise, encouragement, support and approval ... what they desire most.*"

It is worth dying for the truth than sharing in evil and lies. It has become a slogan in Nigeria to say: if you can not beat them, join them: And that is what most Nigerians stood for. But what should be paramount to Christians should be their service to God and humanity and not to –egocentricity. The Bible says that:

> "*Evil men will bow down in the presence of good and the wicked at the gate of the righteous*"(Prov.14:19 ASV.)

Falsehood, strife after money, wealth and power are the ultimate within all the facets of Nigerian politics and lifestyle. Christians should rise up to the challenges before them in the light of the gospel, goodnews.

I agree with Chief Dr. Edet J. Amana who adopted a saying from late Emperor Hailie Selassie which says:

> *"Throughout history, it*
> *is the in-action of those*
> *who could have acted,*
> *the indifference of*
> *those who should have*
> *known better, the*
> *silence of the voice of*
> *justice when it*
> *mattered most that*
> *have made it possible*
> *for evil to triumph."*

The above does mean that Christians should not go into solitary confinement for prayers only but that they should be involved. Being on the fence would not help matters but a deeper involvement is needed. After all, who among the Christians in Nigeria will say that he or she is not affected by the wave of dirty politics and economic morass that is almost destroying and tearing Nigeria apart? When we are personally satisfied with who we —

are and what we have without taking cognizance of others in our society, the love of God does not dwell in us, or our lives. Ours should be that of service to others first.

I am absolutely sure that there is nothing like ethnicity within God's promised mansions – John 14:1 ff. There should be nothing like majority and minority, no coup, no poor or rich, not traditional ruler nor political ruler etc, but for the fact that the earth belongs to God, children of God should be in charge for good. Practically, we snould ignore all that seems to close our ears as Christians about the development around us, our neighbours and the society in general. Christian ethics must be used as the guiding light or measuring rod on how Christians should contribute to the political development of this great country. When any nation is not towing on the right political track or path and is not accepted by the comity of nations, such a country is to fail completely. We have lived with the following in Nigeria over the years;poor economy, collapse of institutions from Primary School to tertiary institutions or the educational sector as a whole, lack of food, housing and electricity supply, poor health care delivery system, a daily rise of inflation and unemployment to mention but a few. While the few rich people are getting richer everyday, the poor are descending into abyss. Christ himself said, "The harvest is great but the labourers are few."

On the final analysis, I have this message from J.O. Ikirodah for all Christians:

> *"If Christians refused to participate in government, the devil and his agents will take over and they, the Christians should not complain."*

Twice in the Royalty Hotel at Eket, Akwa Ibom State through the auspices of Chief Dr. Edet Amana, I was called upon to take opening prayers in political meetings of the Chairmen of Local Government Areas within Eket Senatorial District, and in a meeting of the leadership of United Nigeria Congress Party called "Caucus Dinner." At the first meeting, I spoke on the topic "call to serve and not to be served", and my text was from Matthew 20:25-28. At the second meeting, God led me into talking on the topic, "Accountability in the choice of king or leaders," Deut. 17:14-20. On both occasions I drew the attention of the great men of politics to their duties for their people; on the second occasion I told them of the need to appoint somebody well known to them as a man of integrity and of good character. But the warning remains that if Christians do not want to take part in the act of government let them not complain at all.

I have a great urge that it is not sin for Christians to be spread out in all areas or vocations. The church as an organized body of Christians and the body of Christ must try her best not only through prayers but by involvement to allow her members both lay and clergy to identify with leadership in Nigeria. I am not saying that the church should act as a political party but that the 'church' can help her members to make a right choice of leader. Remember:

"*Righteousness exalts a nation but sin is a disgrace to any people.*" (Prov.14:34 NIV).

When Christians prayed for good government, do they pray to God to send somebody from among the Moslems, Hindu, Traditionalist etc who are good people to lead excluding themselves? I condemn it in a very strong term, loud and clear that it is a sin and a selfish act for

Christians not be involved in the choice or election of who should lead their nation. Prof. N.S.S. Iwe in one of his comments said:

> "Bad officials are elected by good citizens who do not vote."

Furthermore, if politics is the conduct of public affairs and besides the earth belonging to the Lord and the fullness thereof, God fearing people must of necessity be in the leadership. If people who are dirty and evil minded as well as those who are selfish are only those in the game of politics, the game in sincerity cannot but be dirty in its entirety. Christian, you must be involved and denominations should allow those who fear God to take control of what belongs to God. Your involvement will lead to an atmosphere in which the love of God and fellow human beings will be exercised in a nut shell.

Brothers and sisters in Christ Jesus, let us not be misdirected by anyone, while expecting the second coming of the Lord, we can contribute in making the world a better place to an extent for our fellow men. We cannot all be

Pastors and Evangelists, some of us are administrators as given to us by the Holy Spirit. Let us use our talent(s) aright and use same in winning souls into the kingdom of God.

On a final note, I wish to state clearly that Christians' denial of the existence of politics both within and outside the church, that is the act of taking control of leadership in order to achieve a desired goal or ideals, is a lie. My experience as a minister for the past ten years both in the field, tertiary institution and two Theological Institutions have all given me the experience of the fact that 'politics' and 'man' can never be separated. After-all I have in recent times noticed that either individuals or denominations are always struggling one way or the other to out-do the other. Where there is the majority as we have in Trinity Union Theological College, the minority should only be seen and not to be heard. Where it is so done, the majority must put every thing together to frustrate the administration. If one from the majority is leading and does not follow a set up agenda whether for evil or good, such a leader is being fought from all angles or avenues.

The 'therefore' of politics with Christians in Nigeria is that Christians must wake up from their slumber and Luke-warmness towards politics and elections and take their proper places in the scheme of things in order to contribute to make Nigeria a better place and nation. The Duke of Wellington once said, "Educate men without religion and you make them clever devils". The measure of evil an educated man who is not both a Christian or religious could do is that which can never be compared to what an illiterate peasant can ever try to do. Christians are wanted, in almost every endeavour to put things right – medically, legally, educationally, socially, economically, politically etc.

Though we have had some bad examples of failures in political office of executive chairman in my Local Government Area – Urue Offong/Oruko in Akwa Ibom State where professing bornagain, pastor's son and other Christians failed woefully as chairmen except the administration of Hon. Chief Dr. Esio Okwong Udo now member House of Representatives and what the present Chairman – Chief Engr. Etim E. Okon is trying to put in place which the locust had eaten for some years back the truth is that, ' where there is no vision, the people perish or die' Chief Engr. Etim Edet Okon whom I have known for some six years was never in any way associated or affiliated with any religious group or Christian denomination but what he is definitely doing in my Local Government Council in the present political dispensation is amazing. This man's action in office is the type that can always force people to ask "whether being a Christian is the ultimate in doing good things especially things that others could see?"

Perhaps Engr. Chief Etim Edet Okon is emulating the brilliant examples of Hon. Chief (Dr.) Esio O. Udo, now member of the National Assembly, who had performed very well while chairman of my Local Government Area. I clearly and boldly emphasise that others failed woefully, be they elected, selected, imposed or otherwise.

Whereas past administrations sold out Mass Transit buses of the Local Council, to themselves, some re-commissioned a building that was built and commissioned before their administration, and others in trying the best they could to loot the treasury of the council making everything within the council personal, as military dictators, the present man by the grace of God is taking the Council a step forward and should be supported by the Christians. I am also duly convinced that what is our experiences in our Local Council and State is also very similar to what is happening nation-wide.

Christian, remember we shall all render our account before God Almighty and an unbeliever should note that his or her case has been carefully judged.

> "*Whoever believes in him is not condemned,*
> *but whoever does not believe stands condemned*
> *already because he has not believed in the name*
> *of God's one and only son. This is the verdict.*
> *Light has come into the world, but men loved darkness instead of light because their*
> *deeds were evil". Everyone who does evil hates*
> *the light and will not come into the light for*
> *fear that his deeds will be exposed.*

But whoever lives by the truth comes into the light, so that it may be seen plainly that what he has done has been done through God."
(John 3:18-21 NIV.)

We must remember that we have a role to play in changing the lives and condition of others through the word of the gospel. We are not only to win men for Christ but to also make their lives meaningful. I want to remind everyone that when Christ taught the disciples how to pray when they asked for it, He plainly pointed out that they should pray for the will of God to be done on earth as it is in heaven –

"*Our Father in heaven*
hallowed be your name
your kingdom come
your will be done
on earth as it is in heaven"
Matthew 6:10 NIV.

If we asked or prayed four the will of God to be done here on earth as it is in heaven we must be prepared to bring it to pass. That is for God's goodness, sufficiency and power to be manifested in our lives and in the lives of our fellow men – neighbours. Remember that it shall profit a man nothing if he shall gain the whole world and forfeit his soul to hell. It is not all the materials that we acquire here on earth that give joy and peace, it is God the source of all good that gives both. How pleasant it would be for Christians to be actively involved in not just changing the destiny of souls from hell to heaven but by also making this world a better place for mankind.

Remember, if you do not want to elect or be elected, my dear Christian brothers and sisters, you should not complain and be critical of any administration

Remember, if you do not want to elect or be elected, my dear Christian brothers and sisters, you should not complain and be critical of any administration by using vain words which you know you will give account of but just be quiet and fold your hands and watch in silence. But here is what all Christians are sincerely encouraged to do, by Paul:

> "*I urge then, first of all, that requests, prayers, intercession and thanksgiving be made for everyone – for kings and all those in authority, that we may live peaceful and quiet lives in all godliness and holiness. This is good, and*

pleases God our Saviour who wants all men to be saved and to come to a knowledge of the truth."
(1 Timothy 2:1-4 NIV)

May the good God and Jesus Christ his son with the Holy Spirit perfectly guide us to do that which is pleasing in his sight as you join hands in contributing not only spiritually but politically in making this world a better place as we await Christ's second coming for his Church and his people. Amen.

Finally, let us not get ourselves messed up by what Prof., E. M. Uka, in one of his sermons, in Trinity Union Theological College, identified as AIDS – Acquired Integrity Deficiency Syndrome which besieges Nigerians from every imaginable angle or area of life. Brother and sister in the Lord let us take the admonition of St. Paul as recorded in the epistle to the Philippians –

> "*Finally, beloved, whatever is true, whatever is honourable,* whatever is just, whatever is pure, whatever is pleasing, whatever is commendable, if there is any excellence and if there is anything worthy of praise, Think about these things." (Phil.4:8 NRSV.)

"SOME WILL HATE THEE, SOME WILL FLATTER, SOME WILL SLIGHT, CEASE FROM MAN, AND LOOK ABOVE THEE, TRUST IN GOD, AND DO THE RIGHT."

NORMAN MACLEOD 1812-

BIBLIOGRAPHY

Amana, E.J., We Can Take Our People Up There (Lagos – Nigeria: Union Communications and Publications Ltd., 1997).

Barnette, H.H. Introducing Christian Ethics. (Tennessee, U.S.A: Broadman Press, 1961.)

Douglas, J.D.(Ed), The New Bible Dictionary (London, UK: Richard Clay and Co.Ltd., 1963).

Gaub, Ken, Dreams, Plans, Goals: (Arizona, USA: New Leaf Press, 1993).

Haselbarth, H.,Christian Ethics in The African Context (Ibadan, Nigeria: Daystar Press, 1976).

Ikirodah, J.O., Christian in Politics. (Benin, Nigeria:Christian Network Organisation, 1995).

Iwe, N.S.S., Christianity, Culture and Colonialism in Africa. (P.H., Nigeria: College of Education, 1995).

Socio Ethical Issues In Nigeria. (Obosi, Anambra, Nigeria: Pacific College Press, 1991)

Kuitert, H.M., Everything Is Politics But Politics Is Not Everything. (London, UK: S.M.C. Press, 1985).

Kukah, M.H., Religion and Politics of Justice in Nigeria (Lagos, Nigeria: Constitutional Rights Project, 1996).

Iloh, B.(Ed), Macbeth (Essex, England: Longman Group, UK Ltd. 1991).

Mason, John L., Let Go Whatever Makes You Stop. (P.H.Nigeria: Spiritual Life Publications, 1994).

Nnoli, Okwudiba., Ethnic Politics In Nigeria (Enugu, Nigeria: Fourth Dimension Publishing Co.Ltd., 1978).

Nwabueze, B.O. Democratisation. (Ibadan, Nigeria: Spectrum Law Publishing, 1993).

Nwankwo, Arthur A., The Political Transition and The Future of Democracy. (Enugu, Nigeria: Fourth Dimension Co.Ltd., 1993)

Nwaorgu, O.C. Dimensions of Political Analysis. (Lagos, Nigeria: Du Prince Aud Pal, 1998).

O'Donovan, W. Biblical Christianity in African Perspective (U.S.A.: Donneley & Sons Co. 1992).

Okadigbo, Chuba, Power and Leadership in Nigeria. (Enugu, Nigeria: Fourth Dimension Publishing Co.Ltd., 1987).

Osuntokun, A., Power Broker; A Biography of Sir Kasim Ibrahim. (Ibadan, Nigeria: Spectrum Books Ltd. 1987)

Pfeiffer, C. F. & Harrison, E.F. (Eds). The New Testament Wyclife Bible Commentary 5th Edition. (New York, U.S.A.: The Iversen Norman Associates, 1983).

Schuller, Robert H. Tough Times Never Last, But Tough People Do.(Tennessee, U.S.A: Thomas Nelson Inc. 1993

—. Success is Never Ending, Failure Is Never Final (Tennessee, U.S.A.:Thomas Nelson Inc. 1988).

Thiroux, J.P., Ethics: Theory And Practice. (California, U.S.A.: Collier Macmillan Publishers, 1977).

Treat, Casey, Fulfilling Your God Given Destiny. (Tennessee , U.S.A.Thomas Nelson Publishers, 1988).

Yoder, John H. The Politics of Jesus (Ground Rapids, U.S.A: William Berdmans Publishing Company, 1972).

BIBLES

The Amplified Bible (AV).
The Devotional Study Bible (NIV)
New Revised Standard Version (NRSV)
The Study Bible (NIV)
The Revised Standard Version (RSV)
The American Standard Version (ASV)
The Holy Bible (HKJV)

COMMENTS

The book "Christians and Nigerian politics" is a timely guide to all who desire good government for Nigeria and more importantly to all who intend to be part of it. It is a step towards Christians possessing their possessions in governance.
Very Revd. G. A. Agupusi.

"This book is a must for every "Christian Politician." Revd. Canon. Chima Onyebuagu.

"A theo-political distinguished clerical work and gift of the millennium to both Christians and non Christians in Nigeria." Ven. Austin Ugbor.

"The radical evangelization of the political order, is an urgent task for Christians. This book is a useful guide for the accomplishment of the task. It is a step in the right direction. Revd. Uche Kalu Ibe.

ABOUT THE AUTHOR

Revd. Effiong Asuquo Esedeke was born into the family of Mr.Asuquo Esedeke'Reverend' and Mrs.Mayen Asuquo Esedeke at Ukuko-Utuku – 'Blessed People" in Urue Offong/Oruko L.G.A. of Akwa Ibom State, on November 24, 1961. He was brought up in a Christian home since his father because of his activities in the Methodist Church was nicknamed 'Rev: He surrendered his life to Jesus Christ after a wide range of youthful experiences on April 15, 1986 and from that time gave the whole of his time to the service of Christ Church in the Methodist Church Nigeria.

He attended Methodist Central School, Oyubia in Urue Offong/Oruko L.G.A.,Salvation Army Secondary School Akai-Ubium – Nsit Ubium L.G.A. both in Akwa Ibom State, Methodist Theological Institute Umuahia and the University of Calabar where he obtained a B.A. (Hons) degree. He served as a Lecturer and Director of Sports in M.T.I Umuahia and presently a Lecturer at the Trinity Union Theological College, Umuahia and Director of Sports.

Suffice it to say that Revd. Esedeke right from his secondary school days developed interest for politics' and 'good governance', which has culminated in his putting into black and white the problems of Nigerian politics and the way forward. Because of his pragmatic attitude towards the conditions of the people, he is known in some quarters as Reverend Extra-ordinary.

He is happily married to Mrs. Comfort Effiong Esedeke and the marriage is blessed with their miracle son, Onwiabasi Effiong Esedeke.